Objective Quantitative Genetics

DR. PHUNDAN SINGH

Ex-Director

Central Institute for Cotton Research

Nagpur-440 010

KALYANI PUBLISHERS

LUDHIANA • NEW DELHI • NOIDA (UP) • HYDERABAD • CHENNAI

KOLKATA • CUTTACK • GUWAHATI • COCHIN • BENGALURU

KALYANI PUBLISHERS

Head Office

B-1/1292, Rajinder Nagar, **Ludhiana**-141 008 • Ph : 0161-2760031
E-mail : kalyanibooks@yahoo.co.in

Administration Office

4779/23, Ansari Road, **Daryaganj,** New Delhi-110 002
Ph : 011-23271469, 23274393, 23278688 **E-mail :** kalyani_delhi@yahoo.co.in

Works

B-16, Sector-8, **NOIDA** (U.P.)

Branches

1, Mahalakshmi Street, T. Nagar, **Chennai-**600 017 • Ph : 044-24344684
110/111, Bharatia Towers, Badambadi, **Cuttack**-753 009 (Odisha) • Ph : 0671-2311391
3-5-1108, Narayanaguda, **Hyderabad**-500 029 • Ph : 040 24750368
10/2B, Ramanath Mazumdar Street, **Kolkata**-700 009 • Ph : 033-22416024
Arunalaya, 1st Floor, Saraswati Road, Pan Bazar, **Guwahati**-781 001 • Ph : 0361-2731274
Koratti Parambil House, Convent Road, **Cochin**-682 035 • Ph : 0484-2367189
No. 24 & 25, 1st Floor, Hameed Shah Complex, Cubbonpet Main Road, **Bengaluru**-560 002

R-34054 03

First Edition, 2002
Second Revised Edition, 2012

Reprinted, 2021

Typesetting by :
Kalyani Publishers

978-93-272-1795-7

PRINTED IN INDIA

At Kalyani Printings, B-15, Sector-8, Noida (U.P.)
and published by Mrs. Usha Raj Kumar for
Kalyani Publishers, New Delhi-110 002

Dedicated

to

My son

Rajeev Singh

Grand sons

Rishabh Singh, Samrat Choudhary and Shaan Choudhary

and daughter

Ms Pavitra Choudhary

Preface

(Second Edition)

The first edition of this book (Objective Quantitative Genetics) was very well received by the readers (students, teachers and researchers). As a result, the first edition went out of stock soon. I feel immense pleasure in writing preface to second edition of this book. In this edition some changes have been made in light of suggestions received from the esteemed readers. The main change in this edition are as follows :

1. In this edition one chapter "Breeding Value" which is very important in both plant breeding and Animal Breeding has been included.
2. The chapter on Introductory Statistics has been bifurcated in to two chapters, *viz.* Introductory Statistics and Experimental Designs.
3. The sequence of chapters has been changed to make the subject more systematic.
4. There were some printing errors in the first edition which I have attempted to remove in this edition.

My wife Mrs. Jaswanti Singh provided me whole hearted support and cooperation while revising this book for which she deserves special appreciation. I am extremely thankful to Shri Rajkumar, Kalyani Publishers, Ludhiana for reminding me for revision of the book. Hope, this revised edition would be more useful to the students, teachers and researchers engaged in the field of Plant Breeding, Animal Breeding, Plant Genetics and Animal Genetics.

Nagpur **PHUNDAN SINGH**
2012

Preface
(First Edition)

Quantitative genetics is an integral part of plant breeding. Biometrical techniques are widely used in Plant Breeding. Quantitative genetics is taught especially at Post Graduate level in all Agricultural Universities in India and abroad. At university level, students have to answer both descriptive and objective type of questions. There are some books both of foreign and Indian origin on descriptive aspect of quantitative genetics. However, there is hardly any book on the objective aspect.

The present volume "Objective Quantitative Genetics" has been design to fill up this gap. This book contains 18 chapters. Each chapter begins with related definitions and then provides background information about the chapter. The background information helps students in answering objective type questions given in each chapter. Four types of objective questions such as multiple choice, fill in the blanks, true or false and use of appropriate term have been given in each chapter. I have cited a few examples. Teachers and students can frame a lot more such questions for exercise. At the end, valuable information has been appended which can be used to frame additional objective type questions.

My wife Mrs. Jaswanti Singh has provided her fullest cooperation during preparation of this book for which she deserves special appreciation.

This volume covers the course offered at Post Graduate level in different Agricultural Universities of India both in Plant breeding as well as animal breeding. Hope this book would be useful to students and teachers of both plant breeding and animal breeding. This will also be useful for those preparing for various competitive examinations related to plant and animal breeding.

Constructive suggestions of teachers and students are invited for further improvement of this book.

2002 **PHUNDAN SINGH**

Contents

1

CHAPTER

Introduction to Quantitative Genetics

A. DEFINITIONS

Biometrics. The science which deals with the application of statistical concepts and procedures to the study of biological problems.

Biometry. Same as biometrics.

Biostatistics. Same as biometrics or biometry.

Biometrical genetics. A branch of genetics which utilizes statistical concepts and procedures for the study of genetical problems and principles.

Statistical genetics. Since biometrical genetics utilizes various statistical concepts and procedures, it is also referred to as statistical generics.

Mathematical genetics. Since biometrical genetics utilizes various mathematical concepts and procedures, it is also known as mathematical genetics. There are two branches of biometrical genetics, *viz.,* quantitative genetics and population genetics.

Quantitative genetics. A branch of genetics which deals with inheritance and genetic analysis of quantitative or polygen characters.

Biometrical techniques. Various statistical procedures which are used in the study of quantitative genetics.

Population genetics. A branch of genetics which deals with the study of genes in a population and inheritance of oligogenic characters; also called Mendelian genetics

B. BACKGROUND INFORMATION

1. Biometrics is also known as biometry or biostatistics.
2. Biometrical genetics is also termed as Statistical genetics or Mathematical genetics.

3. There are two branches of biometrical genetics, *viz.* Quantitative genetics and Population genetics.
4. Quantitative genetics deals with inheritance of quantitative or polygenic characters.
5. Analysis of quantitative genetics is based on means, variances and covariances.
6. Population genetics is also referred to as Mendelian genetics.
7. Mendelian genetics deals with the study of oligogenic or qualitative traits.
8. The interpretation of Mendelian genetics is based on frequencies and ratios.
9. Quantitative genetics deals with the study of continuous variation.
10. Mendelian genetics deals with discontinuous variation.
11. Quantitative genetics provides ways and means for the study of polygenic traits.
12. Quantitative genetics is an extension of Mendelian genetics firmly based on Mendelian principles of heredity.
13. Quantitative genetics utilizes various statistical models and designs for the analysis of polygenic characters.
14. Quantitative genetics evaluates plant populations in terms of variability, heritability, combining ability, gene action, yield attributes, adaptation etc.
15. Quantitative genetics helps in separation of non-heritable variation from heritable variation
16. Separation of non-heritable variation from heritable variation is not possible in Mendelian genetics.
17. Quantitative genetic estimates are valid for a particular set of environmental conditions and these estimates may change with the change in environment.
18. Quantitative genetic estimates are influenced by several factors such as genetic material, sample size, sampling method, conduct of experiment, method of calculation etc.
19. Biometrical techniques are useful to plant breeder in four principal ways, *viz.*· section of elite genotypes, assessment of polygenic variability, choice of parents and breeding procedures, and assessment of varietal adaptation.
20. Biometrical techniques which are used for assessment of polygenic variation include, measures of disperson, metroglyph analysis, D^2 statistics.
21. Biometrical techniques which help in selection of elite genotypes from diverse genetic populations include correlations, path analysis and discriminant function analysis.
22. Biometrical techniques which help in the selection of parents and breeding procedures include, diallel, partial diallel, line × tester cross, triallel cross and quadriallel cross.
23. Biometrical techniques which help in selection of breeding procedures for genetic improvement of various polygenic characters include, generation mean analysis, biparental cross and triple test cross analysis.
24. Stability analysis helps in the assessment of varietal adaptation.
25. East (1916) demostrated that polygenic characters were perferbly in agreement with Mendelian segregation.

26. Fisher (1918) provided initial frame of biometrics for the study of quantitative genetics.

27. Fisher (1918) divided the genetic variance into additive, dominance and epistatic components.

28. Three biometrical techniques, *viz.* diallel, partial diallel and line × tester are used for evaluation of several single crosses for combining ability variances and effects.

29. Three biometrical techniques, *viz.* generation mean analysis, biparental cross and triple test cross are used for analysis of individual cross in terms of components of genetic variance.

30. Three biometrical techniques, *viz.* diallel, partial diallel and line × tester crosses are known as mating designs.

31. Important books authored by R.A. Fisher and Frank Yates are (*i*) Statistical Tables for biological, agricultural and medical research, and (*ii*) Experimental designs.

32. The important books written by Karl Pearson are : (*i*) Tables for statisticions and biometricians, (*ii*) Tables of incomplete gamma function, and (*iii*) Tables for incomplete beta function.

33. The important book authored by Federer is Experimental Designs—Theory and Applications.

34. Important books authored by Oscar Kempthorne are : (*i*) The Designs and Analysis of Experiments (1952) and (*ii*) An Introduction to Genetic Statistics (1957).

35. The important book authored by K. Mather and J.L. Jinks (1971) is Biometrical Genetics.

36. The famous book authored by D.S. Falconer (1960) is 'Introduction to Quantitative Genetics.'

37. The book authored by C.R. Rao (1952) is Advanced Statistical Methods in Biometrical Research.

38. The important book authored by R.K. Singh and B.D. Choudhary is Biometrical Methods in Quantitative Genetic Analysis.

39. The important book "Biometrical Techniques in Plant Breeding" has been authored by P. Singh and S.S. Narayanan in 1993.

40. A hand book of Agricultural Statistics has been authorod by SBS Chandel (1965).

C. MULTIPLE CHOICE

1. Application of statistical concepts and procedures to the study of biological problems is called :

   (a) Biometrics (b) Biometry
   (c) Biostatistics (d) All of these.

2. Polygenic variation is studied in :

   (a) Biometrical genetics (b) Quantitative genetics
   (c) Statistical genetics (d) All of these.

3. Biometrical genetics is also known as :

   (a) Statistical genetics (b) Mathematical genetics
   (c) Quantitative genetics (d) All of these.

4. Oligogenic Variation is studied in :
(a) Quantitative genetics (b) Mendelian genetics
(c) Population genetics (d) (b) and (c).

5. Initial frame of biometrics for the study of quantitative genetics was provided in 1918 by :
(a) Sir Galton (b) Sir R.A. Fisher
(c) K. Mather (d) D.S. Falconer.

6. Quantitative genetics deals with inheritance of :
(a) Polygenic character (b) Quantitative character
(c) Metrical trait (d) All of these.

7. Analysis of quantitative genetics is based on :
(a) Means (b) Variances
(c) Covariances (d) All of these.

8. The interpretation of Mendelian genetics is based on :
(a) Frequencies (b) Genetic ratios
(c) (a) and (b) (d) Mean values.

9. Quantitative genetics provides information about :
(a) Variability (b) Heritability
(c) Gene action (d) All of these.

10. Quantitative genetic estimates are influenced by :
(a) Genetic material (b) Sample size
(c) Sampling method (d) All of these.

11. Polygenic variation can be assessed through :
(a) Metroglyph analysis (b) D^2 statistics
(c) Measures of dispersion (d) All of these.

12. Yield components can be determined by :
(a) Correlation analysis (b) Path analysis
(c) Discriminant function (d) All of these.

13. Several single crosses can be evaluated at a time for combining ability variances and effects by :
(a) Diallel cross (b) Partial diallel cross
(c) Line × tester cross (d) All of these.

14. Individual cross can be evaluated for components of genetic variance by :
(a) Generation mean analysis (b) Biparental cross
(c) Triple test cross (d) All of these.

15. Which of the following biometrical techniques is called Mating design ?
(a) Diallel cross (b) Partial diallel cross
(c) Line × tester cross (d) All of these.

16. Who demonstrated that polygenic characters are perfectly in agrement with Mendelian segregation ?
(a) East (b) Shull
(c) Mather (d) Fisher.

17. Choice of suitable parents for use in the hybridization programme particularly for development of single cross hybrid can be made by :

(a) Diallel analysis
(b) Partial diallel analysis
(c) Line × testor cross
(d) All of these.

18. Parents for development of double cross hybrid can be selected by :

(a) Triallel analysis
(b) Quadriallel analysis
(c) Generation mean analysis
(d) Triple test cross analysis.

19. Parents for development of three way cross hybrid can be selected through :

(a) Diallel analysis
(b) Partial diallel analysis
(c) Triallel analysis
(d) Quadriallel analysis.

20. Suitable breeding procedure can be decided through :

(a) Diallel, partial diallel and line × tester analysis
(b) Generation mean, biparental cross and triple test cross analysis
(c) Triallel and Quadriallel analysis
(d) All of these.

21. The similarity between polygenic and oligogenic characters was first demostrated by East in :

(a) 1908
(b) 1916
(c) 1921
(d) 1935.

22. The book "Tables for Statisticians and Biometricians" was written by :

(a) R.A. Fisher
(b) K. Mather
(c) Karl Pearson
(d) None of these.

23. The famous Statistical Tables for "Biological, Agricultural and Medical Research" was authored by :

(a) Mather and Jinks
(b) Fisher and Yates
(c) Hayman
(d) Karl Pearson.

24. Who wrote the famous book "Experimental Designs" ?

(a) Fisher and Yates
(b) Jinks and Jones
(c) Mather and Jinks
(d) None of these.

25. The book "Designs and Analysis of Experiments" was written in 1952 by .

(a) R.A. Fisher
(b) Frank Yates
(c) Oscar Kempthorne
(d) D.S. Falconer.

26. The famous book "An Introduction to Genetic Statistics" was written in 1957 by :

(a) Sir Galton
(b) R.A. Fisher
(c) Oscar Kempthorne
(d) K. Mather.

27. The famous book "Biometrical Genetics" was first written in 1949 by :

(a) R.A. Fisher
(b) K. Mather
(c) Frank Yates
(d) Sir Galton.

28. The revised edition of the book "Biometrical Genetics" was written in 1971 by :

(a) Fisher and Yate
(b) Mather and Jinks
(c) Jinks and Jones
(d) D.S. Falconer.

29. The famous book "Introduction to Quantitative Genetics" was written in 1960 by :

(a) K. Mather (b) D.S. Falconer

(c) Oscar Kempthorne (d) J.L. Jinks.

30. The book "Advanced Statistical Methods in Biometrical Research" was authored by :

(a) Panse and Sukhatme (b) C.R. Rao

(c) Nageshwar Rao (d) R.K. Singh.

31. The famous books "Biometrical Methods in Quantitative Genetic Analysis' was authored in 1976 by :

(a) C.R. Rao (b) Nageshwar Rao

(c) Singh and Choudhary (d) C.R. Rao.

32. The important book "Biometrical Techniques in Plant Breeding" was authored in 1993 by :

(a) Singh and Choudhary (b) Panse and Sukhatme

(c) Singh and Narayanan (d) C.R. Rao.

33. A Handbook of Agricultural Statistics was authored in 1965 by :

(a) Panse and Sukhatme (b) S.R.S. Chandel

(c) Nageshwar Rao (d) None of these.

34. Which of the following books was written by K. Mather in 1949 :

(a) Biometrical Genetics

(b) Introduction to Quantitative Genetics

(c) Experimental Designs

(d) Designs and Analysis of Experiments.

35. Which of the following books was authored by D.S. Falconer in 1960 :

(a) Introduction to Quantitative Genetics

(b) Designs and Analysis of Experiments

(c) An Introduction to Genetic Statistics

(d) Biometrical Genetics.

D. FILL IN THE BLANKS

1. Biometrics is also called ....

2. Biometrical genetics is also known as ....

3. .... genetics deals with inheritance of polygenic traits.

4. .... genetics deals with inheritance of oligogenic traits.

5. Population genetics is also known as ....

6. Mendelian genetics deals with inheritance of ....traits.

7. Continuous variation is studied in ....

8. Discontinuous variation is studied in ....

9. Quantitative genetics is an extension of ....

10. The initial frame of biometrics was provided by ....

11. Fisher provided initial frame of biometrics in ....

12. The genetic variance was divided into additive, dominance and epistatic components by ....
13. Analysis of .... genetics is based on means, variances and covariances.
14. Interpretation .... genetics is based on frequencies and ratios.
15. The book Biometrical Genetics was written by ....
16. The famous book Introduction to Quantitative Genetics was authored by ....
17. The book Advanced Statistical Methods in Biometrical Research was written by ....
18. The book an Introduction to Genetic Statistics was written by ....
19. The book Tables for Statisticians and Biometricians was written by ....
20. The book Statistical Tables for Biological, Agricultural and Medical Research was written by ....
21. Famous book the Designs and Analysis of Experiments was written by ....
22. "A Handbook of Agricultural Statistics" was written by ....

E. MARK TRUE OR FALSE

1. Quantitative genetics deals with inheritance of oligogenic characters.
2. Quantitative genetics is also called Statistical or Mathematical genetics.
3. Analysis of quantitative genetics is based on frequencies and ratios.
4. Quantitative genetics deals with the study of continuous variation.
5. Initial frame of biometrical genetics was provided by Galton.
6. Biometrics is also called Biometry.
7. Quantitative genetics is an extension of Mendelian genetics.
8. Fisher divided genetic variance into additive, dominance and epistatic components.
9. Additive variance is non-fixable.
10. Dominance variance is fixable.
11. D^2 and metroglyph analysis are called Classificatory techniques.
12. Corrolations, path and selection indices help in determining yield components.
13. Diallel and line × tester techniques are called mating designs.
14. Generation means, biparental cross and triple test cross techniques evaluate several crosses at a time.
15. Triallel and quadriallel analysis donot provide information about epistatic variance.
16. Diallel, partial diallel and line × testor techniques provide estimates of combining ability.
17. The book Biometrical Genetics was written by Fisher.
18. The book "An Introduction to Quantitative Genetics" was authored by Falconer.
19. The book "An Introduction to Genetic Statistics" was written by Kempthorne.
20. The book "Tables for Statisticians and Biometricians" was written by Fisher and Yates.

F. USE APPROPRIATE TERM

1. The science dealing with application of statistical concepts and procedures to the study of biological problems.
2. A branch of genetics that utilizes statistical concepts and procedures for the study of genetical problems.
3. A branch of genetics which deals with the inheritance of polygenic characters.
4. A branch of genetics which deals with the inheritance of oligogenic characters.
5. Various statistical procedures which are used in the study of quantitative genetics.
6. Several genes governing the same character.

ANSWERS

MULTIPLE CHOICE

1. (d) All of these
2. (d) All of these
3. (d) All of these
4. (d) (b) and (c)
5. (b) Sir R.A. Fisher
6. (d) All of these
7. (d) All of these
8. (c) (a) and (b)
9. (d) All of these
10. (d) All of these
11. (d) All of these
12. (d) All of these
13. (d) All of these
14. (d) All of these
15. (d) All of these
16. (a) East
17. (d) All of these
18. (b) Quadriallel analysis
19. (c) Triallel analysis
20. (d) All of these
21. (b) 1916
22. (c) Karl Pearson
23. (b) Fisher and Yates
24. (a) Fisher and Yates
25. (c) O. Kempthorne
26. (c) O. Kempthorne
27. (b) K. Mather
28. (b) Mather and Jinks.
29. (b) D.S. Falconer
30. (b) C.R. Rao
31. (c) Singh and Choudhary
32. (c) Singh and Narayanan
33. (b) S.R.S. Chandel
34. (a) Biometrical genetics
35. (a) Introduction to quantitative genetics.

FILL IN THE BLANKS

1. Biometry, biostatistics
2. Statistical/Mathematical genetics
3. Quantitative
4. Mendelian
5. Mendelian genetics
6. Oligogenic
7. Quantitative genetics
8. Mendelian genetics
9. Mendelian genetics
10. Fisher
11. 1918
12. Fisher
13. Quantitative
14. Mendelian
15. Mather
16. Falconer
17. C.R. Rao

18. Kempthorne
19. Pearson
20. Fisher and Yates
21. Kempthorne
22. Chandel

TRUE OR FALSE

1. False **2.** True **3.** False
4. True **5.** False **6.** True
7. True **8.** True **9.** False
10. False **11.** True **12.** True
13. True **14.** False **15.** False
16. True **17.** False **18.** True
19. True **20.** False

APPROPRIATE TERM

1. Biometrics
2. Biometrical genetics
3. Quantitative genetics
4. Mendelian genetics
5. Biometrical techniques
6. Polygenes

2

CHAPTER

Polygenic and Oligogenic Characters

A. DEFINITIONS

Character. Any property of an individual showing heritable variation. It includes morphological, physiological, biochemical and behavioural properties. Characters are of two types, *viz.* Oligogenic character and Polygenic character.

Oligogenic character. Characters which are controlled by one or few genes each gene having detectable individual effect. Such characters exhibit discontinuous or discrete variation. Oligogenic characters are also called major gene characters or qualitative characters.

Oligogenes. One or few major genes governing the same character.

Oligogenic inheritance. The mode of inheritance of qualitative characters.

Polygenes. Several genes governing the same character.

Polygenic trait. Characters which are governed by several genes each gene having small undetectable individual effect. Such characters exhibit continuous variation; also called quantitative characters or minor gene characters.

Polygenic inheritance. The inheritance of polygenic character; also called quantitative inheritance or Multiple-factor inheritance.

Contributing alleles. Those alleles which contribute to continuous variation; also called effective alleles.

Non-contributing alleles. Those alleles which do not contribute to continuous variation; also called non-effective alleles.

Transgressive segregation. The phenomenon through which we get variation in F_2 or later generation outside the range of both the parents.

Transgressive segregants. Segregants which fall outside the range (limits) of both the parents for a character.

Free variability. Phenotypic differences between homozygotes with extreme phenotypes (AABBCC and aabbcc).

Potential variability. Variability which is bound or hidden in the heterozygotes (AaBb) or homozygotes (AAbb or aaBB) which do not have the extreme phenotype.

Heterozygotic potential variability. The variability which is stored in heterozygote *e.g.* AaBb.

Homozygotic potential variability. The variability which is stored in homozygotes. *viz.* AAbb or aaBB.

B. BACKGROUND INFORMATION

1. The term polygene was coined by Mather in 1941.
2. In quantitatic characters, the effect of individual gene is small which is not easily detectable.
3. Polygenic characters are also called quantitative characters or minor gene characters.
4. Polygenic characters exhibit continuous variation from one extreme to other, hence their classification into different clearcut groups is not possible.
5. Polygenic characters are highly sensitive to environmental changes.
6. Polygenic characters are measured in terms of height, lengths, width, weight, duration etc.
7. Transgressive segregation is possible in case of polygenic characters.
8. Transgressive segregants are obtained only from crosses between two parents having mean values for a polygenic trait.
9. The analysis of polygenic characters is based on means, variances and covariances.
10. Mather (1943) recognized two types of variability for polygenic characters, *viz.* free variability and potential variability.
11. The potential variability is stored in the form of linked polygenic complexes (AaBbCc or AABBcc or aaBBCC or AAbbcc etc.)
12. The hidden variability is released after inter-mating of such genotypes with other genotypes.
13. The linkage among polygenes leads to slow release of potential variability.
14. Quantitative characters exhibit discontinuous variation, hence classification into clear cut groups is impossible.
15. Qualitative characters are also known as oligogenic character, major gene characters, monogenic characters.
16. In case of qualitative characters, effect of each gene is large and easily detectable.
17. In qualitative charaters, gene action is primarily of non-additive type (dominance and epistasis).
18. Qualitative characters are more stable to environmental changes.
19. Qualitative characters do not show transgressive segregation.

20. Analysis of qualitative characters is based on frequencies and segregation ratios.
21. Qualitative characters are measured in terms of colour, shape, surface of various plant parts.
22. Mutation, segregation and linkage are common features of both qualitative and quantitative characters.
23. In plant breeding, both qualitative and quantitative characters have equal economic importance.
24. Quantitative characters are expressed in terms of degree rather than kind.
25. Almost all plant parts and function exhibit differences of quantitative nature.

C. MULTIPLE CHOICE

1. Which of the following properties of an individual is considered heritable ?
   (a) Morphological (b) Physiological
   (c) Biochemical (d) All of these.
2. Qualitative character is also called :
   (a) Major gene character (b) Oligogenic trait
   (c) Monogenic trait (d) All of these.
3. Quantitative character is also known as :
   (a) Minor gene character (b) Polygenic character
   (c) Variable character (d) All of these.
4. Polygenic trait is also termed as :
   (a) Quantitative character (b) Multiple factor character
   (c) Minor gene character (d) All of these.
5. The term Polygenic was coined in 1941 by :
   (a) Fisher (b) Mather
   (c) Hayman (d) None of these.
6. Mather coined the term polygene in :
   (a) 1921 (b) 1935
   (c) 1941 (d) 1957.
7. Oligogenic characters are governed by :
   (a) One gene (b) Few genes
   (c) Several genes (d) (a) and (b) above.
8. Polygenic characters are governed by :
   (a) Few genes (b) Single gene
   (c) Several genes (d) All of these.
9. Transgressive segregants fall outside the limits of :
   (a) Male parent (b) Female parent
   (c) Both parents (d) None of these.
10. Polygenic variability was classified into free and potential variability by :
   (a) Wright (b) Mather
   (c) Hayman (d) Falconer.

11. Mather classified polygenic variation into free and potential variability in :
(a) 1918 (b) 1921
(c) 1943 (d) 1957.

12. Hiden (potential) variability from homozygotes is released by :
(a) Selfing (b) Inbreeding
(c) Outcrossing (d) All of these.

13. Potential variability from heterozygotes is released by :
(a) Selfing (b) Inbreeding
(c) (a) and (b) (d) Outcrossing.

14. Analysis of polygenic traits is based on :
(a) Means (b) Variances
(c) Covariances (d) All of these.

15. Analysis of oligogenic characters is based on :
(a) Variances (b) Covariances
(c) Means (d) Frequencies.

16. Oligogenic characters are measured in terms of :
(a) Colour (b) Shape
(c) Surface (d) All of these.

17. Polygenic traits are measured in terms of :
(a) Height and weight (b) Length and width
(c) Duration (d) All of these.

18. Common features of oligogenic and polygenic characters include :
(a) Linkage (b) Segregation
(c) Mutation (d) All of these.

19. Major gene character refers to :
(a) Monogenic character (b) Oligogenic character
(c) Qualitative character (d) All of these.

20. Minor gene character refers to :
(a) Quantitative character (b) Polygenic character
(c) (a) and (b) (d) Oligogenic character.

21. Which of the following traits exhibit continuous variation ?
(a) Oligogenic (b) Monogenic
(c) Polygenic (d) None of these.

22. Which of the following trait exhibits discontinuous variation ?
(a) Oligogenic (b) Monogenic
(c) Quantitative (d) All of these.

23. Clear cut grouping into different classes is possible for :
(a) Monogenic character (b) Oligogenic character
(c) Quantitative character (d) All of these.

24. Clear cut classification into different groups is not possible in case of :
(a) Oligogenic character (b) Polygenic character
(c) Major gene character (d) All of these.

25. Which of the following traits is more sensitive to environmental changes ?

(a) Quantitative
(b) Qualitative
(c) Polygenic
(d) (a) and (c) above.

D. FILL IN THE BLANKS

1. The term polygene was coined by ....

2. Mather first used the term polygene in ....

3. The term oligogene was first used by ....

4. Polygenic characters are also known as ....

5. Oligogenic characters are also called ....

6. Major gene characters refer to .... character.

7. Minor genic traits refer to .... characters.

8. .... characters exhibit continuous variation.

9. .... characters exhibit discontinuous variation.

10. Transgressive segregation is possible in case of .... traits.

11. .... characters are highly sensitive to environmental changes.

12. The analysis of .... character is based on means, variances and covariances.

13. .... characters are little influenced by environmental variation.

14. Effect of individual gene is distinct and easily detectable in case of .... characters.

15. Effect of individual gene is not easily detectable in case of .... characters.

16. Classification of .... character is possible into clear cut groups.

17. .... characters cannot be classified into clear cut groups.

18. Analysis of .... is based on frequencies and segregation ratios.

19. .... characters are measured in terms of shape, size and colour.

20. Metric measurement is possible in case of .... characters.

21. Metric measurement is not possible in case of .... characters.

22. .... characters are expressed in terms of .... rather than kind.

E. MARK TRUE OR FALSE

1. Terms oligogene and polygenes were coined by Mather.

2. Polygenic character exhibit discontinuous variation.

3. Oligogenic character exhibit continuous variation.

4. Polygenic characters are also called quantitative traits.

5. Oligogenic characters are also known as qualitative characters.

6. Polygenic characters are governed by minor genes.

7. Oligogenic characters are governed by major genes.

8. Metric measurement is not possible for polygenic characters.

9. Metric measurement is possible for oligogenic traits.
10. Polygenic traits are less sensitive to environmental variation.
11. Oligogenic characters are more sensitive to environmental variation.
12. Clear cut classification into different groups in possible in case of oligogenic characters.
13. Analysis of polygenic characters is based on means, variances and covariances.
14. Transgressive segregation is possible in case of oligogenic traits.
15. Quantitative characters express in kind.
16. Qualitative characters express in degree.
17. Effect of individual gene is distinct in case of oligogenic characters.
18. Effect of individual gene is not easily detectable in case of polygenic characters.
19. Inheritance of oligogenic character is studied in quantitative genetics.
20. Inheritances of polygenic characters is studied in Mendelian genetics.

F. USE APPROPRIATE TERM

1. Any property of an individual showing heritable variation.
2. Character controlled by one or few genes each gene having detectable individual effect.
3. One or few genes governing the same character.
4. The mode of inheritance of quantitative characters.
5. Characters which are governed by several genes each gene having small undetectable individual effect.
6. Several genes governing the same character.
7. The inheritance of polygenic character.
8. The phenomenon through which we get segregants which fall outside the range of both the parents for a character.
9. Phenotypic differences between homozygotes with extreme phenotypes (AABBCC and aabbcc).
10. Variability which is hidden in heterozygotes.

ANSWERS

MULTIPLE CHOICE

1. (d) All of these
2. (d) All of these
3. (d) All of these
4. (d) All of these
5. (b) Mather
6. (c) 1941
7. (a) One gene
8. (c) Several genes
9. (c) Both parents
10. (b) Mather
11. (c) 1943
12. (c) Outcrossing
13. (c) (a) and (b)
14. (d) All of these
15. (d) Frequencies
16. (d) All of these
17. (d) All of these

18. (d) All of these
19. (d) All of these
20. (c) (a) and (b)
21. (c) Polygenic
22. (c) Qualitative
23. (d) All of these
24. (b) Polygenic character
25. (c) Polygenic

FILL IN THE BLANKS

1. Mather
2. 1941
3. Mather
4. 1941
5. Quantitative characters
6. Qualitative characters
7. Quantitative
8. Quantitative
9. Qualitative
10. Polygenic/quantitative
11. Polygenic
12. Polygenic
13. Oligogenic
14. Oligogenic
15. Polygenic
16. Oligogenic
17. Polygenic
18. Oligogenic
19. Oligogenic
20. Polygenic
21. Oligogenic
22. Polygenic

TRUE OR FALSE

1. True	**2.** False	**3.** False
4. True	**5.** True	**6.** True
7. True	**8.** False	**9.** False
10. False	**11.** False	**12.** True
13. True	**14.** False	**15.** False
16. False	**17.** True	**18.** True
19. False	**20.** False	

APPROPRIATE TERM

1. Character
2. Oligogenic characters
3. Oligogenes
4. Oligogenic inheritance
5. Polygenic characters
6. Polygenes
7. Polygenic inheritance
8. Transgressive segregation
9. Free variability
10. Potential variability

●●●

3

CHAPTER

Assessment of Polygenic Variation

A. DEFINITIONS

Variability. Presence of differences among the individuals of a population due to differences in their genetic constitution or the environment in which they are grown or more likely both. The polygenic variation present in the plant population is of three types, *viz.* phenotypic, genotypic and environmental.

Phenotypic variation. The total variability which is observable. It is measured in terms of phenotypic variance.

Genotypic variation. The inherent or genetic variability which remains unaltered by environmental conditions. It is measured in terms of genotypic variance.

Environmental variation. Non-heritable variation which is entirely due to environmental effects. This uncontrolled variation is measured in terms of error mean variance.

Genetic diversity. Total amount of genetic variation present in a population or species or variety of genes and genotypes found in a particular crop species.

Genetic erosion. Loss of genetic diversity between and within population of a species over a period of time.

Metroglyph analysis. A semigraphic method of studying variability in large number of germplasm lines or segregating populations at a time.

D^2 Statistics. A statistical procedure which is used to measure the genetic diversity in a population. It measures the inter-and intracluster variation and measures the relative contribution of each component trait to the total divergence.

Cluster diagram. A line diagram which is used in D^2 statistics to depict the genetic diversity.

Glyph. In metroglyph analysis a small circle which depicts the position of a genotype on the graph.

B. BACKGROUND INFORMATION

1. Burton (1952) divided the polygenic variation into phenotypic, genotypic and environmental components.
2. Polygenic variation was first interpreted in terms of Mendelian genetics by R.A. Fisher (1918).
3. There are three methods of assessing polygenic variation, *viz.* (1) Simple measures of variability (range, standard deviation, variance, standard error and coefficient of variation), (2) Metroglyph analysis and (3) D^2 statistics.
4. Metroglyph analysis was developed by Anderson in 1957 to investigate the pattern of morphological variation within a crop species or among germplasm lines.
5. Analysis of metroglyph is based on first order statistics and therefore, results are statistically more reliable and robust.
6. Metroglyph analysis is possible from both replicated and unreplicated data.
7. In metroglyph technique, the pattern of variability is depicted by glyphs on the graph.
8. In metroglyph technique, the maximum score of an individual will be $3n$, where n is the number of characters included in the study.
9. With n characters, the minimum score of a genotype in metroglyph analysis would be n.
10. Metroglyph analysis is useful in classification of germplasm for various characters.
11. The concept of D^2 statistics was originally developed by P.C. Mahalanobis in 1928.
12. Use of D^2 statistics for assessment of genetic diversity in plant breeding was first suggested by C.R. Rao in 1952.
13. Estimates of D^2 statistics are based on second order statistics.
14. D^2 statistics is useful in identification of divergent parents for use in the hybridization programmes.
15. The analysis of D^2 statistics is possible from replicated data only.
16. In D^2 analysis, the genetic diversity is depicted by the cluster diagram.
17. Number of clusters represent the number of groups in which a population can be classified on the basis of D^2 statistics.
18. The distance between two clusters is the measure of the degree of diversification. The greater the distance between two clusters the greater the divergence and *vice-versa*.
19. Genotypes falling in the same cluster are less divergent than those placed in different clusters.
20. Metroglyph and D^2 statistics have some common features such as both are classificatory techniques, free from genetical assumptions and provide measures of variability and genetic diversity.
21. Variability in the populations is important for disease resistances, adaptability and effective selection.

22. Land races have more genetic diversity, resistance to biotic and abiotic stresses, wide adaptability and broad genetic base.
23. Modern varieties have narrow genetic base poor adaptability and danger of uniformity.
24. In nature genetic variability is maintained by spontaneous mutations, outcrossing and recombinations.
25. Use of multiline varieties and land races helps in controlling disease epidemics.

C. MULTIPLE CHOICE

1. Polygenic variation includes :
   (a) Phenotypic variation (b) Genotypic variation
   (c) Environmental variation (d) All of these.
2. Phenotypic variance includes :
   (a) Genotypic variance (b) Error variance
   (c) (a) and (b) (d) None of these.
3. Phenotypic variation is measured in terms of :
   (a) Genotypic variance (b) Phenotypic variance
   (c) Error variance (d) None of these.
4. Genotypic variation is measured in terms of :
   (a) Error variance (b) Phenotypic variance
   (c) Genotypic variance (d) All of these.
5. Genotypic variation consists of :
   (a) Additive variance (b) Dominance variance
   (c) Epistatic variance (c) All of these.
6. Error variance is a measure of :
   (a) Genotypic variation (b) Phenotypic variation
   (c) Environmental variation (d) None of these.
7. Polygenic variation is assessed by :
   (a) Measures of disperson (b) D^2 statistics
   (c) Metroglyph analysis (d) All of these.
8. Cluster diagram is related to :
   (a) Path analysis (b) D^2 statistics
   (c) Metroglyph analysis (d) All of these.
9. Glyph is related to :
   (a) D^2 statistics (b) Diallel analysis
   (c) Metroglyph analysis (d) Path analysis.
10. Polygenic variation was divided into phenotypic, genotypic and environmental components in 1952 by :
   (a) Mather (b) Fisher
   (c) Burton (d) Hayman.
11. Polygenic variation was first interpreted in terms of Mendelian genetics in 1918 by :
   (a) Sewall Wright (b) R.A. Fisher
   (c) K. Mather (d) D.S. Falconer.

12. The concept of metroglyph analysis was developed in 1957 by :
(a) P.C. Mahalanobis (b) Anderson
(c) Burton (d) Wright.

13. Anderson developed the concept of metroglyph analysis in :
(a) 1918 (b) 1921
(c) 1957 (d) 1962.

14. Analysis of metroglyph analysis is based on :
(a) Mean values (b) Variances
(c) Covariances (d) All of these.

15. Which degree of statistics is involved in the analysis of metroglyph technique ?
(a) First degree (b) Second degree
(c) Third degree (d) All of these.

16. In metroglyph analysis with n characters, maximum score of a genotype would be :
(a) n (b) $2n$
(c) $3n$ (d) $4n$.

17. The concept of D^2 statistics was developed in 1928 by :
(a) Anderson (b) Burton
(c) Mahalanobis (d) Fisher.

18. Mahalanobis developed the concept of D^2 statistics in :
(a) 1918 (b) 1921
(c) 1928 (d) 1949.

19. Use of D^2 statistics for assessment of genetic diversity in plant breeding was first suggested in 1952 by :
(a) P.C. Mahalanobis (b) C.R. Rao
(c) Anderson (d) Fisher.

20. C.R. Rao suggested the use of D^2 statistics for assessment of genetic diversity in plant breeding in :
(a) 1928 (b) 1936
(c) 1952 (d) 1957.

21. Which degree of statistics is involved in the D^2 analysis ?
(a) First order (b) Second order
(c) Third order (d) All of these.

22. In D^2 statistics, the genetic variability is depicted by :
(a) Vr-Wr graph (b) Glyphs
(c) Cluster diagram (d) All of these.

23. In plant breeding population, variability is important for :
(a) Disease resistance (b) Adaptability
(c) Effective selection (d) All of these.

24. Land races have :
(a) Genetic diversity (b) Wide adaptability
(c) Broad genetic base (d) All of these.

25. Modern cultivars have :

(a) Narrow genetic base (b) Uniformity
(c) Poor adaptability (d) All of these.

26. In nature, variability is maintained by :

(a) Spontaneous mutations (b) Outcrossing
(c) Recombinations (d) All of these.

D. FILL IN THE BLANKS

1. Polygenic variation was divided into phenotypic, genotypic and environmental components by ....

2. Polygenic variation was first interpreted in terms of Mendelian genetics by ....

3. Metroglyph analysis was proposed by ....

4. Metroglyph analysis was developed in ....

5. Analysis of metroglyph analysis is based on .... statistics.

6. Metroglyph analysis can be done from .... data.

7. Glyph is related to .... analysis.

8. With *n* characters, the minimum score of a genotype in metroglyph analysis would be ....

9. The concept of D^2 statistics was developed by ....

10. P.C. Mahalanobis developed the concept of D^2 statistics in ....

11. Use of D^2 statistics in plant breeding was first suggested by ....

12. C.R. Rao suggested use of D^2 statistics for assessment of genetic diversity in plant breeding populations in ....

13. Estimates of D^2 are based on .... statistics.

14. Cluster diagram is related to ....

15. D^2 analysis is possible from .... data.

16. In D^2 analysis, the genetic diversity is depicted by ....

17. The distance between two clusters is the measure of the degree of ....

18. D^2 analysis helps in identification of .... parents.

19. Genotypes falling in the same cluster are ....

20. Genotypes falling in different clusters are ....

E. MARK TRUE OR FALSE

1. Fisher divided polygenic variation into genotypic, phenotypic and environmental components.

2. Fisher first provided interpretation of polygenic variation in terms of Mendelian genetics.

3. Metroglyph analysis was proposed by Smith.

4. Metroglyph analysis was developed in 1940.

5. Metroglyph analysis can be done with unreplicated data.

6. Analysis of metroglyph is based on second degree statistics.
7. Metroglyph analysis is a classificatory technique.
8. In metroglyph technique, variation is depicted with the help of glyph on the graph.
9. The concept of D^2 statistics was developed by Anderson.
10. Concept of D^2 statistics was developed in 1957.
11. C.R. Rao first suggested use of D^2 statistics in plant breeding.
12. D^2 statistics helps in assessment of genetic diversity in the breeding populations.
13. D^2 statistics is free from genetic assumptions.
14. Metroglyph analysis is based on some genetical assumptions.
15. D^2 analysis is possible from unreplicated data.
16. In D^2 analysis, genetic diversity is depicted by cluster diagram.
17. D^2 analysis helps in determining yield components.
18. Divergent parents can be identified with the help of D^2 analysis.
19. Less divergent genotypes fall in different clusters.
20. More divergent genotypes fall in the same cluster.

F. USE APPROPRIATE TERM

1. Presence of genetic differences among the individuals of a population.
2. Total variability which is observable.
3. The inherent or genetic variability which remains unaltered by environmental conditions.
4. Non-heritable variation which is entirely due to environmental effects.
5. Variety of genes and genotypes found in a species.
6. Loss of genetic diversity between and within population of a species over a period of time.
7. A semigraphic method of studying variability in large number of germplasm lines at a time.
8. A statistical technique which is used to measure genetic diversity at intra and inter cluster levels.
9. A line diagram which is used in D^2 statistics to depict the genetic diversity.
10. In metroglyph analysis, a small circle which depicts the variation of a genotype on the graph.

ANSWERS

MULTIPLE CHOICE

1. (d) All of these
2. (c) (a) and (b)
3. (b) Phenotypic variance
4. (c) Genotypic variance
5. (d) All of these
6. (c) Environmental variation
7. (d) All of these
8. (b) D^2 statistics
9. (c) Metroglyph analysis

10. (c) Burton
11. (b) R.A. Fisher
12. (b) Anderson
13. (c) 1957
14. (a) Mean values
15. (a) First degree
16. (c) 3*n*
17. (c) Mahalanobis
18. (c) 1928
19. (b) C.R. Rao
20. (c) 1952
21. (c) Third order
22. (c) Cluster diagram
23. (d) All of these
24. (d) All of these
25. (d) All of these
26. (d) All of these

FILL IN THE BLANKS

1. Burton
2. Fisher
3. Anderson
4. 1957
5. First order
6. Unreplicated
7. Metroglyph
8. *n*
9. Mahalanobis
10. 1928
11. C.R. Rao
12. 1952
13. Second order
14. D^2 statistics
15. Unreplicated
16. Cluster diagram
17. Diversification
18. Divergent
19. Less divergent
20. More divergent.

TRUE OR FALSE

1. False	**2.** True	**3.** False
4. False	**5.** True	**6.** False
7. True	**8.** True	**9.** False
10. False	**11.** True	**12.** True
13. True	**14.** False	**15.** False
16. True	**17.** False	**18.** True
19. False	**20.** False.	

APPROPRIATE TERM

1. Variability
2. Phenotypic variation
3. Genotypic variation
4. Environmental variation
5. Genetic diversity
6. Genetic erosion
7. Metroglyph analysis
8. D^2 statistics
9. Culster diagram
10. Glyph

●●●

4

CHAPTER

Correlations in Plant Breeding

A. DEFINITIONS

Correlation coefficient. A statistical measure which is used to find out the degree and direction of relationship between two or more variables. It is represented by r and is of three types, *viz.* simple, partial and multiple.

Simple correlation. The association between any two variables; also called total correlation or zero order correlation. It is of three types *viz.* phenotypic, genotypic and environmental.

Phenotypic correlation. The association between two variables which can be directly observed. It is worked out from phenotypic variances and covariances.

Genotypic correlation. The inherent or heritable correlation between two variables; also called genetic correlation. It is estimated from genotypic variances and covariances.

Environmental correlation. The association between two variables which is entirely due to environmental effects. It is estimated from error variances and covariances.

Negative correlation. The correlation in which increase in one variable leads to decrease in other variable and *vice-versa.*

Positive correlation. The correlation in which increase in one variable leads to increase in other variable and *vice-versa.*

Partial correlation. Estimation of correlation between two variables eliminating the effect of third variable; also called net correlation. It is represented as $r_{12.3}$. It is of two types. *viz.* first order partial correlation and second order partial correlation.

First order partial correlation. The partial correlation which is estimated from simple correlations and involves three variables. It is denoted as $r_{12.3}$.

Second order partial correlation. Partial correlation which is estimated from first order partial correlations and involves four variables. It is represented as $r_{12.34}$.

Multiple correlation. Joint influence of two or more independent variables on a dependent variable. It is denoted as $R_{1.23.}$

Coefficient of determination. The square of multiple correlation coefficient *i.e.* R^2.

B. BACKGROUND INFORMATION

1. Correlation is independent of the unit of measurement.
2. The value of correlation lies between – 1 and 1.
3. Simple correlation is also known as total correlation or zero order correlation.
4. Simple correlation involves two variables.
5. Simple correlation is represented as r.
6. The value of simple correlation is always lower than multiple correlation.
7. Phenotypic correlation is denoted as rph.
8. Genotypic correlation is denoted as rg.
9. Environmental correlation in represented as re.
10. Genotypic correlation may be either due to pleiotropic action of genes or due to linkage or more likely both.
11. All possible combinations of correlation among n variables are equal to $n\ (n–1)/2$.
12. Partial correlation involves three or four variables.
13. Partial correlations are estimated from simple correlations.
14. First order partial correlation is denoted as $r_{12.3}$.
15. Second order partial correlation is denoted as $r_{12.34}$
16. The value of partial correlation is always lower than multiple correlation.
17. Multiple correlation involves several variables.
18. Multiple correlation is represented as $R_{1.23}$.
19. Multiple correlation is estimated from simple correlations.
20. The value of multiple correlation is always higher than simple and partial correlations.
21. Coefficient of determination can be obtained directly from multiple correlation.
22. The value of multiple correlation is always positive. It varies between 0 and 1.
23. Genotypic correlation is more stable than phenotypic correlation.
24. Simple, partial and multiple correlations can be estimated from both unreplicated and replicated data.
25. Phenotypic, genotypic and environmental correlations can be estimated from replicated data only.
26. Simple correlation is calculated as $\dfrac{\text{cov}_{xy}}{\sqrt{\text{var}\ x\ .\ \text{var}\ y}}$.
27. Phenotypic correlation is estimated as $\dfrac{\text{Pcov}_{xy}}{\sqrt{\text{Pv}_x\ .\ \text{Pv}_y}}$.

28. Genotypic correlation is worked out as $\frac{\text{Gcov}_{xy}}{\sqrt{\text{Gv}_x \, . \, \text{Gv}_y}}$.

29. Environmental correlation is estimated as $\frac{\text{Ecov}_{xy}}{\sqrt{\text{Ev}_x \, . \, \text{Ev}_y}}$.

30. Partial correlation (first order) is estimated as : $r_{12.3} = r_{12} - r_{13} r_{23} \sqrt{(1 - r_{13}^2)(1 - r_{13}^2)}$.

31. Multiple correlation is estimated as follows : $\text{R}_{1.23} = \frac{(r_{12}^2 + r_{13}^2 - 2r_{12}.r_{13}.r_{23})}{\sqrt{(1 - r_{23}^2)}}$.

C. MULTIPLE CHOICE

1. Simple correlation is also known as :

(a) Total correlation (b) Zero order correlation
(c) (a) and (b) (d) None of these.

2. Simple correlation is represented as :

(a) r_{12} (b) $r_{12.3}$
(c) $r_{1.23}$ (d) $\text{R}_{1.23}$.

3. Partial correlation is denoted as :

(a) $r_{12.3}$ (b) $r_{1.23}$
(c) $\text{R}_{1.23}$ (d) $\text{R}_{12.3}$.

4. Partial correlation is also referred to as :

(a) Total correlation (b) Zero order correlation
(c) Net correlation (d) All of these

5. The phenotypic correlation is represented as :

(a) r_g (b) r_{ph}
(c) $r_{12.3}$ (d) $\text{R}_{1.23}$

6. The genotypic correlation is represented as :

(a) $r_{12.3}$ (b) r_g
(c) *rph* (d) R^2.

7. The environmental correlation is denoted as :

(a) *rg* (b) *rph*
(c) *re* (d) $\text{R}_{1.23}$.

8. Phenotypic variances and covariances are used for the estimation of :

(a) Genotypic correlation (b) Phenotypic correlation
(c) Environmental correlation (d) All of these.

9. Genotypic variances and covariances are used for the estimation of :

(a) Environmental correlation (b) Genotypic correlation
(c) Phenotypic correlation (d) None of these.

10. Environmental variances and covariances are used for the estimation of :
(a) Genotypic correlation (b) **Environmental correlation**
(c) Phenotypic correlation (d) **Multiple correlation.**

11. Second order partial correlation is represented as :
(a) $r_{12.3}$ (b) $r_{12.34}$
(c) r_{12} (d) $R_{1.23}$.

12. First order partial correlation is represented as :
(a) $r_{12.3}$ (b) r_{12}
(c) $r_{12.34}$ (d) R^2.

13. The coefficient of determination is represented as :
(a) $R_{12.3}$ (b) R^2
(c) $r_{12.3}$ (d) r_{12}.

14. The coefficient of determination can be directly obtained from :
(a) Simple correlation (b) Partial correlation
(c) Multiple correlation (d) All of these.

15. The value of simple correlation lies between :
(a) 0 and 1 (b) 1 and 2
(c) –1 and 1 (d) None of these.

16. The value of partial correlation is always lower than :
(a) Simple correlation (b) Genotypic correlation
(c) Phenotypic correlation (d) Multiple correlation.

17. The value of multiple correlation is always :
(a) Negative (b) Positive
(c) Zero (d) None of these.

18. The value of multiple correlation lies between :
(a) –1 and 1 (b) 1 and 2
(c) 0 and 1 (d) None of these.

19. Which of the following correlations is more stable ?
(a) Genotypic (b) Phenotypic
(c) Environmental (d) All of these.

20. Genotypic correlation is also known as :
(a) Inherent correlation (b) Heritable correlation
(c) Genetic correlation (d) All of these.

21. Genotypic correlation results due to :
(a) Pleiotropy (b) Linreage
(c) (a) and (b) (d) Gene interaction.

22. The formula $cov_{xy}/\sqrt{var_x \cdot var_y}$ is used for the estimation of :
(a) Simple correlation (b) Partial correlation
(c) Multiple correlation (d) All of these.

23. The formula $Pcov_{xy}/\sqrt{Pv_x.Pv_y}$ is used for the estimation of :

(a) Genotypic correlation (b) Phenotypic correlation
(c) Environmental correlation (d) None of these.

24. The formula $Gcov_{xy}/\sqrt{Gv_x.Gv_y}$ is used for the estimation of :

(a) Phenotypic correlation (b) Genotypic correlation
(c) Partial correlation (d) Multiple correlation.

25. The formula $r_{12} - r_{13}.r_{23}/\sqrt{(1-r_{13}^2)(1-r_{13}^2)}$ is used for calculation of :

(a) Simple correlation (b) Partial correlation
(c) Multiple correlation (d) Genotypic correlation.

26. R^2 denotes :

(a) Simple correlation (b) Partial correlation
(c) Multiple correlation (d) Coefficient of determination.

27. *rg* denotes :

(a) Partial correlation (b) Genotypic correlation
(c) Phenotypic correlation (d) None of these.

28. The formula $\dfrac{(r_{12}^2 + r_{12}^2 - 2r_{12}.r_{13}.r_{23})}{\sqrt{(1-r_{23}^2)}}$ is used for estimation of :

(a) Simple correlation (b) Multiple correlation
(c) Partial correlation (d) None of these.

29. *rph* denotes :

(a) Partial correlation (b) Multiple correlation
(c) Phenotypic correlation (d) Genotypic correlation.

30. *re* denotes :

(a) Genotypic correlation (b) Environmental correlation
(c) Phenotypic correlation (d) None of these.

31. In plant breeding, correlations are used for determining :

(a) Gene action (b) Segregation pattern
(c) Yield components (d) Dominance pattern.

D. FILL IN THE BLANKS

1. The correlation is independent of the unit of ....
2. The value of correlation lies between .... and ....
3. Simple correlation is also called ....
4. Simple correlation is represented as ....
5. Phenotypic correlation is represented as ....
6. Genotypic correlation is represented as ....
7. Environmental correlation is denoted as ....

8. Partial correlation is also called ....
9. First order partial correlation is denoted as ....
10. Second order partial correlation is represented as ....
11. Multiple correlation is represented as ....
12. The value of multiple correlation is always ....
13. The value of multiple correlation lies between .... and ....
14. R^2 refers to ....
15. The square of multiple correlation is called ....
16. Multiple correlation is estimated from ....
17. Simple correlation is estimated as ....
18. Phenotypic correlation is estimated as ....
19. Genotypic correlation is calculated as ....
20. Environmental correlation is calculated as ....
21. Simple correlation involves .... variables.
22. Partial correlation involves .... variables.
23. Multiple correlation involves .... variables.
24. The inherent correlation refers to ....

E. TRUE OR FALSE

1. The value of correlation lies between 0 and 1.
2. The simple correlation is represented as R.
3. The simple correlation is also called net correlation.
4. The partial correlation is denoted as $r_{12.3}$.
5. The partial correlation is also called total correlation.
6. The zero order correlation refers to simple correlation.
7. The value of partial correlation is always lower than multiple correlation.
8. The second order partial correlation is denoted as $r_{12.34}$.
9. Genotypic correlation results due to linkage, pleiotopy or both.
10. The genotypic correlation is non-heritable.
11. The environmental correlation is heritable.
12. Genotypic correlation is also called inherent corrolation.
13. The value of simple correlation is always higher than multiple correlation.
14. Simple correlation involves three or more variables.
15. Partial correlation involves two variables.
16. Multiple correlation is denoted as R.
17. Multiple correlation is always positive.
18. The value of multiple correlation lies between 0 and 1.

19. The value of multiple correlation is always lower than simple and partial correlation.
20. The R^2 refers to coefficient of determination.
21. Multiple correlation is estimated from simple correlation.
22. Correlation is expressed in the unit of measurement of the character.

F. USE APPROPRIATE TERM

1. A statistical measure of the degree and direction of relationship between two or more variables.
2. The association between two variables.
3. The observable association between two variables.
4. The inherent correlation between two variables.
5. Association between two variables which is entirely due to environmental effects.
6. Association in which increase in one variable leads to decrease in other variable and *vice-versa*.
7. Association in which increase in one variable leads to increase in other variable and *vice-versa*.
8. Estimation of correlation between two variables eliminating the effect of third variable.
9. The partial correlation that involves three variables.
10. The partial correlation that involves four variables.
11. Joint influence of two or more independent variables on a dependent variable.
12. The square of multiple correlation.

ANSWERS

MULTIPLE CHOICE

1. (c) (a) and (b)
2. (a) r_{12}
3. (a) $r_{12.3}$
4. (c) Net correlation
5. (b) *rph*
6. (b) *rg*
7. (c) *re*
8. (b) Phenotypic correlation
9. (b) Genotypic correlation
10. (b) Environmental correlation
11. (b) $r_{12.34}$
12. (a) $r_{12.3}$
13. (b) R^2
14. (c) Multiple correlation
15. (c) –1 and 1
16. (d) Multiple correlation
17. (b) Positive
18. (c) 0 and 1
19. (a) Genotypic
20. (d) All of these
21. (c) (a) and (b)
22. (a) Simple correlation
23. (b) Phenotypic correlation
24. (b) Genotypic correlation
25. (b) Partial correlation
26. (d) Coefficient of determination
27. (b) Genotypic correlation
28. (b) Multiple correlation
29. (c) Phenotypic correlation
30. (b) Environmental correlation
31. (c) Yield components.

Fill in the Blanks

1. Measurement
2. –1, 1
3. Total or Zero order correlation
4. *r*
5. *rph*
6. *rg*
7. *re*
8. Net correlation
9. $r_{12.3}$
10. $r_{12.34}$
11. R
12. Positive
13. 0, 1
14. Coefficient of determination
15. Coefficient of determination
16. Simple correlations
17. $\text{Cov}_{xy}/\sqrt{\text{var}_x \, . \, \text{var}_y}$
18. $\text{Pcov}_{xy}/\sqrt{\text{Pv}_x . \text{Pv}_y}$
19. $\text{G cov}_{xy}/\sqrt{\text{Gv}_x . \text{Gv}_y}$
20. $\text{Ecov}_{xy}/\sqrt{\text{Ev}_x \, . \, \text{Ev}_y}$
21. Two
22. Three or more
23. Several
24. Genetic correlation

TRUE OR FALSE

1. False	2. False	3. False
4. True	5. False	6. True
7. True	8. True	9. True
10. False	11. False	12. True
13. False	14. False	15. False
16. True	17. True	18. True
19. False	20. True	21. True
22. False.		

APPROPRIATE TERM

1. Correlation coefficient
2. Simple correlation
3. Phenotypic correlation
4. Genotypic correlation
5. Environmental correlation
6. Negative correlation
7. Positive correlation
8. Partial correlation
9. First order partial correlation
10. Second order partial correlation
11. Multiple correlation
12. Coefficient of determination

●●●

5

CHAPTER

Path Coefficient Analysis

A. DEFINITIONS

Path analysis. A standardized partial regression coefficient which splits the correlation coefficient into the measures of direct and indirect effects. Thus, it measures the direct and indirect contribution of various independent variables on the dependent variable. Path coefficients are of three types, *viz.* phenotypic, genotypic and environmental.

Phenotypic path. Path coefficient which is estimated from all possible phenotypic correlations among different variables.

Genotypic path. Path coefficient which is measured from all possible genotypic correlations among different variables.

Environmental path. Path coefficient which is estimated from all possible environmental correlations among different variables.

Path diagram. In path analysis, a line diagram which is constructed to depict the cause and effect situation. Path analysis estimates direct effects, indirect effects and residual effect.

Direct effect. Straight effect of an independent variable on dependent variable.

Indirect effect. Effect of an independent variable on dependent variable via other variables (characters).

Residual effect. A measure of other possible variables (characters) which have not been included in the study.

Direct selection. Straight selection for dependent character for example selection for yield per se.

Indirect selection. Selection for a component tract for improving economic yield.

B. BACKGROUND INFORMATION

1. The concept of path coefficient analysis was originally developed by Sewall Wright (1921).
2. Path coefficient technique was first used for plant selection in 1959 in Crested Wheatgrass.
3. Path analysis measures the cause of association between two variables.
4. Analysis of path coefficient is based on all possible simple correlations among various characters.
5. Path analysis is based on the assumptions of linearity and additivity.
6. Path analysis measures direct effect, indirect effect and residual effect.
7. Path analysis helps in determining yield components.
8. Path analysis is useful for improvement in yield through indirect selection.
9. Phenotypic path is estimated from phenotypic correlations.
10. Genotypic path is estimated from genotypic correlations.
11. Environmental path is worked out from environmental conditions.
12. Path diagram is constructed with the help of all possible simple correlations among various characters under study.
13. Path diagram is constructed before estimation of direct and indirect effects.
14. For path analysis, dependent character, say yield, is kept at one side and all independent variables (characters) on the other side.
15. Path diagram provides visual picture of cause and effect situation.
16. Path diagram helps in setting up of simultaneous equations.
17. The formula $n(n-1)/2$ is used for deciding all possible simple correlations among in variables (characters).
18. Direct effects are estimated by solving simultaneous equations.
19. Indirect effects are estimated by using values of direct effects and correlation coefficients.
20. The residual effect is estimated with the help of all direct effects and correlations of independent variables with dependent one.
21. The formula $I = P^2R_5 + P_{15}.r_{15} + P_{25}.r_{25} + P_{35}.r_{35} + P_{45}.r_{45}$ is used for estimation of residual effect using five variables.
22. Scales for path coefficient analysis were proposed by Lenka and Mishra (1973) working with rice.
23. Path analysis provides basis for selection of superior genotypes from the diverse breeding populations.
24. It is quite possible that a character showing positive direct effect on yield may have a negative indirect effect via other component traits.
25. The values of direct and indirect effects are classified as neglible (0.00-0.09), low (0.10-0.19), moderate (0.20-0.29), high (0.30-0.99) and very high (above 1).

26. The sum of direct and indirect effects of an independent character gives value of its correlation with dependent character, say yield.

27. Straight selection for yield per se is called direct selection.

28. Improvement of yield by making selection for a component character is called indirect selection.

C. MULTIPLE CHOICE

1. The concept of Path coefficient analysis was developed in 1921 by :
(a) Sewall Wright (b) K. Mather
(c) R.A. Fisher (d) D.S. Falconer.

2. Sewall Wright developed the concept of path coefficient analysis in :
(a) 1918 (b) 1921
(c) 1949 (d) 1960.

3. Path coefficient was first used for plant selection in 1959 by :
(a) Smith (b) Mather
(c) Dewey and Lu (d) Falconer.

4. Dewey and Lu first used path coefficient analysis in :
(a) 1918 (b) 1936
(c) 1951 (d) 1959.

5. Path coefficient technique was first used for genetic improvement of :
(a) Maize (b) Rice
(c) Crested wheatgrass (d) Sorghum.

6. Path analysis estimates :
(a) Direct effects (b) Indirect effects
(c) Residual effects (d) All of these.

7. Genotypic path is estimated directly from :
(a) Genotypic variance (b) Genotypic covariance
(c) Genotypic correlations (d) All of these.

8. Phenotypic path is estimated directly from :
(a) Phenotypic covariance (b) Phenotypic correlations
(c) Phenotypic covariance (d) None of these.

9. Environmental path is estimated directly from :
(a) Genotypic variance (b) Phenotypic covariance
(c) Environmental correlations (d) All of these.

10. Genotypic correlations are used for estimating :
(a) Genotypic path (b) Phenotypic path
(c) Environmental path (d) All of these.

11. Path analysis is based on the assumptions of :
(a) Linearity (b) Additivity
(c) (a) and (b) (d) None of these.

12. In plant breeding, path analysis is done for determining :
(a) Gene action (b) Linkage
(c) Yield components (d) All of these.

13. Path analysis helps in improving yield through :
(a) Direct selection (b) Indirect selection
(c) Recurrent selection (d) All of these.

14. Path diagram is constructed by using values of :
(a) Correlations (b) Direct effects
(c) Indirect effects (d) Residual effects.

15. Path diagram is constructed before estimation of :
(a) Direct effects (b) Indirect effects
(c) Residual effects (d) All of these.

16. All possible simple correlations among n variables are equal to :
(a) $n(n + 1)/2$ (b) $n(n - 1)/2$
(c) n^2 (d) $n(n + 1)$.

17. If the value of direct and indirect effect lies between 0.30-0.99, it is considered as :
(a) Low (b) Moderate
(c) High (d) Very high.

18. Scales for path analysis were provided by :
(a) Smith (b) Wright
(c) Dewey and Lu (d) Lenka and Mishra.

19. Which of the following is related to path analysis ?
(a) Vr-Wr graph (b) Metroglyph chart
(c) Cluster diagram (d) Path diagram.

20. The formula $I = P^2R_5 + P_{15}.r_{15} + P_{25}.r_{25} + P_{35}.r_{35} + P_{45}.r_{45}$ is used for estimation of :
(a) Correlation (b) Direct effect
(c) Indirect effect (d) Residual effect.

21. All possible phenotypic corrolations among n variables are required for estimation of :
(a) Genotypic path (b) Phenotypic path
(c) Environmental path (d) All of these.

22. The estimation of environmental path is based on :
(a) Environmental correlations (b) Simple correlations
(c) Partial correlations (d) None of these.

23. How many assumptions are involved in path analysis :
(a) Two (b) Three
(c) Four (d) Five.

24. Path diagram provides information about :
(a) Variability (b) Gene action
(c) Cause and effect (d) All of these.

D. FILL IN THE BLANKS

1. The concept of path analysis was developed in ....
2. Concept of path analysis was developed by ....
3. Path analysis was first used for plant selection by ....
4. Dewey and Lu first used path analysis in ....
5. Path analysis was first used in .... crop.
6. Path analysis measures .... between two variables.
7. Path analysis is a modified form of ....
8. Path analysis is done from all possible .... among *n* variables.
9. Path analysis is based on the assumptions of ....
10. Path analysis helps in determining .... components.
11. Phenotypic path is estimated from ....
12. Genotypic path is estimated from ....
13. Environmental path is estimated from ....
14. Path diagram is constructed with the help of all possible simple ....
15. Path diagram provides visual picture of .... situation.
16. Path diagram helps in setting up of ....
17. Direct effects are estimated by solving ....
18. The formula $I = P^2R_5 + P_{15}.r_{15} + P_{25}.r_{25} + P_{35}.r_{35} + P_{45}.r_{45}$ is used for estimation ....
19. The values of direct effects and correlation coefficients are used for estimating ....
20. The scales of direct and indirect effects were proposed by ....
21. Straight selection for yield per se is called ....
22. Improvement of yield by making selection for a component selection is called ....
23. Path analysis provides basis for .... of superior plants.
24. All possible simple correlations among *n* variables are equal to ....

E. MARK TRUE OR FALSE

1. The concept of path analysis was developed in 1930.
2. The concept of path analysis was developed in Fisher.
3. Path analysis was first used for plant selection by Dewey and Lu.
4. Dewey and Lu first used path analysis in Soybean.
5. For plant selection path analysis was first used in 1959.
6. Path analysis is a modified form of standardised partial regression coefficient.
7. All possible simple correlation coefficient are used for estimation of path coefficient.
8. Path analysis is free from statistical assumptions.
9. Path analysis provides basis for selection.
10. Path analysis provides information about yield components.

11. Phenotypic correlations are used for estimating genotypic path.
12. Genotypic correlations are used for estimating phenotypic path.
13. Environmental path is estimated from environmental correlations.
14. Path diagram is constructed with the help of variances and covariances.
15. Path diagram provides clear picture of cause and effect situation.
16. Path diagram helps in setting up of simultaneous equations.
17. By solving simultaneous equations, values of direct effects can be obtained.
18. Path diagram is constructed before estimation of direct and indirect effects.
19. Path analysis helps in indirect selection.
20. The scales for direct and indirect effects were proposed by Lenka and Mishra (1973).

F. USE APPROPRIATE TERM

1. A statistical technique that splits the correlation coefficient into the measure of direct and indirect effects.
2. Path which is estimated from all possible phenotypic correlations among n characters.
3. Path that is estimated from all possible genotypic correlations among n characters.
4. Path that is estimated from all possible environmental correlations among n characters.
5. In path analysis, a line diagram that is constructed to depict the cause and effect situation.
6. Straight effect of an independent variable on the dependent variable.
7. Effect on an independent variable on dependent variable via other variables.
8. A measure of other possible variables (characters) which have not been included in the path analysis.
9. Straight selection for dependent character, say for yield.
10. Selection for a component character for improving yield.

ANSWERS

MULTIPLE CHOICE

1. (a) Sewall Wright
2. (b) 1921
3. (c) Dewey and Lu
4. (d) 1959
5. (c) Crested Wheatgrass
6. (d) All of these
7. (c) Genotypic correlations
8. (b) Phenotypic correlations
9. (c) Environmental correlations
10. (a) Genotypic path
11. (c) (a) and (b)
12. (c) Yield components
13. (b) Indirect selection
14. (a) Correlations
15. (d) All of these
16. (b) $n(n-1)/2$
17. (d) Very high
18. (d) Lenka and Mishra
19. (d) Path diagram
20. (d) Residual effect
21. (d) All of these
22. (a) Environmental correlations
23. (a) Two
24. (c) Cause and effect.

FILL IN THE BLANKS

1. 1921
2. Wright
3. Dewey and Lu
4. 1959
5. Crested Wheatgrass
6. Cause and effect
7. Standardized partial regression
8. Simple correlations
9. Linearity and additivity
10. Yield
11. Phenotypic correlations
12. Genotypic correlations
13. Environmental correlations
14. Correlations
15. Cause and effect
16. Simultaneous equations
17. Simultaneous equations
18. Residual effect
19. Indirect effects
20. Lenka and Mishra
21. Direct selection
22. Indirect selection
23. Selection
24. $n(n-1)/2$

TRUE OR FALSE

1. False	2. False	3. True
4. False	5. True	6. True
7. True	8. False	9. True
10. True	11. False	12. False
13. True	14. False	15. True
16. True	17. True	18. True
19. True	20. True	

APPROPRIATE TERM

1. Path analysis
2. Phenotypic path
3. Genotypic path
4. Environmental path
5. Path diagram
6. Direct effect
7. Indirect effect
8. Residual effect
9. Direct selection
10. Indirect selection

6

CHAPTER

Discriminant Function

A. DEFINITIONS

Discriminant function. A statistical procedure which is used in constructing selection index and discriminates desirable genotypes from undesirable ones based on various character combinations.

Selection index. A linear combination of plant characters which is associated with yield. Selection index is of three types, *viz.* classical selection index, restricted selection index and general selection index.

Classical selection index. A type of selection index which involves several characters in selection index simultaneously and discriminates between desirable and undesirable genotypes on the basis of selection efficiency.

Restricted selection index. A type of selection index which helps in improving a set of characters keeping the value of other characters intact. Sometimes the restriction is put on one character and sometimes on double characters.

General selection index. A type of selection index in which weights for various traits are based on the average value for several populations. This is modified form of classical selection index.

Weighing coefficients. The relative importance of various characters in the selection index.

Relative efficiency. A measure of the effectiveness of various selection indices. It is the percentage ratio of genetic advance for discriminant function (GS_1) to genetic advance for direct selection (GS_2).

GS_1. Genetic advance for discriminant function which is estimated separately for various selection indices involving single, double, triple and multiple traits.

GS_2. Genetic advance by direct method which is calculated for dependent character (yield) only.

B. BACKGROUND INFORMATION

1. The concept of discriminant function analysis was developed by H.F. Smith (1936).
2. The use of discriminant function for plant selection was first proposed by Smith in 1936.
3. In discriminant function analysis, based on various characters associated with yield, an index is constructed which is called selection index.
4. Selection index is of three types, *viz.* classical, general and restricted.
5. The classical selection index was proposed by Smith in 1936. This index discriminates between desirable and undesirable genotypes based on selection efficiency.
6. General selection index was proposed by Hanson and Johnson in 1957. It is a modified form a classical selection index.
7. Restricted selection index was proposed by Kempthorne and Nordskog in 1959.
8. In animal improvement, discriminant function analysis was first used by Hazel in 1943.
9. This technique measures the efficiency of various character combinations in plant selection.
10. Selection index leads to simultaneous manipulation of several characters for genetic improvement of economic yield.
11. The analysis of discriminant function involves variances and covariances. In other words, analysis of this technique is based on variances and covariances.
12. Analysis of this technique is based two statistical assumptions, *viz.* linearity and additivity.
13. In this technique, weight coefficients, expected genetic advance and relative selection efficiency are estimated.
14. The construction of selection index is based on six genetical assumptions, *viz.*, (*i*) diploid segregation (*ii*) lack of maternal effects, (*iii*) absence of linkage, (*iv*) absence of epistasis, (*v*) absence of multiple alleles, and (*vi*) equal survival of all genotypes in a population.
15. Construction of all types of selection indices is based on the estimates of phenotypic and genotypic variances and covariances of the characters involved in the selection index.
16. Construction of selection index requires three parameters, *viz.*, weight coefficients, expected genetic advance and relative selection efficiency.
17. The relative efficiency is worked out separately for various selection indices involving single, double and multiple traits.
18. Relative efficiency measures the effectiveness of various selection indices.
19. The relative efficiency of direct selection for yield is considered as 100%.
20. Any selection index showing higher relative efficiency than direct selection is considered important and characters involved in such index are considered as major components of yield.
21. Robinson *et al.*, (1951) applied selection index in maize for genetic improvement of grain yield.

22. Brim *et al.* (1959) applied selection index in soybean for genetic improvement of oil yield.

23. Selection indices are not in wide spread use in plant breeding.

24. The general formula of a selection index is as follows :

$$I = b_1X_1 + b_2X_2 + b_3X_3 + \dots b_nX_n$$

where x_1, x_2 x_3 and x_n are phenotypic values of character number, 1, 2, 3 and n, and b_1, b_2, b_3 and b_n are the corresponding weights.

C. MULTIPLE CHOICE

1. The concept of discriminant function analysis was developed in 1936 by :
(a) Fisher (b) Smith
(c) Hazel (d) Mather.

2. Use of discriminant function technique for plant selection was first proposed by :
(a) Mather (b) Fisher
(c) Smith (d) Hazel.

3. Smith proposed discriminant function analysis in :
(a) 1921 (b) 1936
(c) 1943 (d) 1954.

4. The selection index proposed by Smith is known as :
(a) General (b) Classical
(c) Restricted (d) None of these.

5. The classical selection index was proposed by :
(a) Hazel (b) Smith
(c) Jinks and Jones (d) Mather and Jinks.

6. The Restricted selection index was proposed by :
(a) Jinks and Jones (b) Kempthorne and Nordskog
(c) Smith (d) Mather.

7. The General selection index was proposed by :
(a) Hanson and Johnson (b) Kempthorne and Nordskog
(c) Mather (d) Smith.

8. Which of the following selection indices was proposed by Hanson and Johnson in 1957 :
(a) Classical (b) General
(c) Restricted (d) None of these.

9. The Restricted selection index was proposed by Kempthorne and Nordskog in :
(a) 1936 (b) 1943
(c) 1957 (d) 1959.

10. The discriminant function for animal improvement was first used by :
(a) Smith (b) Hazel
(c) Hayman (d) Hanson and Johnson.

11. How many statistical assumptions are to be fulfiled for construction of selection index :
(a) Two (b) Three
(c) Four (d) Five.

12. How many genetical assumptions should be fulfilled for construction of selection index :

(a) Three (b) Four
(c) Five (d) Six.

13. Construction of selection index requires :

(a) Weight coefficients (b) Expected genetic advance
(c) Relative efficiency (d) All of these.

14. The relative efficiency for direct selection of yield is considered as :

(a) 50% (b) 75%
(c) 100% (d) 120%.

15. In plant breeding, which of the following models of selection index is used more than others ?

(a) General index (b) Classical index
(c) Restricted index (d) General and restricted indices.

16. The theory of selection index has been properly developed for the index which was proposed by :

(a) Hanson and Johnson (b) Kempthorne and Nordskog
(c) Smith (d) Hazel.

17. Robinson *et al.* (1951) applied selection index for genetic improvement of grain yield in :

(a) Wheat (b) Barley
(c) Maize (d) Sorghum.

18. Who used selection index for improvement of grain yield in maize :

(a) Smith *et al.* (b) Johnson *et al.*
(c) Robinson *et al.* (d) Mather *et al.*

19. In soybean, selection index for improvement of oil yield was applied by :

(a) Anderson *et al.* (b) Robinson *et al.*
(c) Smith (d) Brim *et al.*

20. In which crop, Brim *et al.* (1959) used selection index for improvement of oil yield :

(a) Mustard (b) Groundnut
(c) Soybean (d) Sesame

D. FILL IN THE BLANKS

1. The concept of discriminant function was developed by ....
2. Smith developed the concept of discriminant function in ....
3. Use of discriminant function for plant selection was first proposed by ....
4. Discriminant function for plant selection was first used in ....
5. The classical selection index was proposed by ....
6. Classical selection index was proposed by Smith in ....
7. General selection index was proposed by ....
8. Hanson and Johnson proposed general selection index in ....

9. Restricted selection index was proposed by ....
10. Kempthorne and Nordskog proposed restricted selection index in ....
11. .... first used discriminant selection for animal improvement.
12. Hazel applied discriminant function for animal improvement in ....
13. Analysis of discriminant function involves ....
14. Construction of selection indices is based on .... statistics.
15. Construction of selection index is based on .... statistical assumptions.
16. Construction of selection index is based on .... genetical assumptions.
17. Relative efficiency measures the effectiveness of various ....
18. The relative efficiency of direct selection for yield is considered ....
19. Robinson *et al.,* (1951) applied selection index in ....
20. In soybean, selection index was applied by ....

E. MARK TRUE OR FALSE

1. The concept of discriminant function was first developed by Wright.
2. The classical selection index was proposed by Smith.
3. Selection index for plant selection was first used in 1927.
4. The General selection index was proposed by Smith and Jinks.
5. The Restricted selection index was proposed by Kempthorne and Nordskog.
6. Restricted selection index was proposed in 1959.
7. Hazel first applied discriminant function for animal improvement.
8. Hazel used discriminant function in 1943 for animal improvement.
9. Construction of selection index is free from genetical assumptions.
10. Construction of selection index is based on two statistical assumptions *i.e.,* linearity and additivity.
11. Construction of selection index is based on third order statistics.
12. Variances and covariances are used in the construction of selection index.
13. The value of relative efficiency for direct selection is considered 100%.
14. The selection index of Smith is widely used.
15. Relative efficiency measures the effectiveness of various selection indices.
16. Selection indices are not in wide spread use in plant breeding.
17. Weight coefficient refers to relative importance of various characters in the selection index.
18. In soybean, selection index was first applied by Robinson *et al.*
19. In maize, selection index was first applied by Brim *et al.*
20. Weight coefficients are represented as b_1, b_2, b_3, ...b_n.

F. USE APPROPRIATE TERM

1. A statistical procedure which is used in constructing selection index and discriminates desirable genotypes from undesirable ones based on various character combinations.

2. A linear combination of plant characters which is associated with yield.
3. A type of selection index which discriminates between desirable and undesirable genotypes based on selection efficiency.
4. A type of selection index which helps in improving a set of characters keeping the value of other characters infact.
5. A type of selection index in which weights for various traits are based on the average value for several populations.
6. Relative importance of various characters in the selection index.
7. A measure of the effectiveness of various selection indices.
8. Genetic advance for discriminant function.
9. Genetic advance calculated by direct method for dependent character.

ANSWERS

MULTIPLE CHOICE

1. (b) Smith
2. (c) Smith
3. (b) 1936
4. (b) Classical
5. (b) Smith
6. (b) Kempthorne and Nordskog
7. (a) Hanson and Johnson
8. (b) General
9. (d) 1959
10. (b) Hazel
11. (a) Two
12. (d) Six
13. (d) All of these
14. (c) 100%
15. (b) Classical index
16. (c) Smith
17. (c) Maize
18. (c) Robinson *et al.*
19. (d) Brim *et al.*
20. (c) Soybean

FILL IN THE BLANKS

1. Smith
2. 1936
3. Smith
4. 1936
5. Smith
6. 1936
7. Hanson and Johnson
8. 1957
9. Kempthorne and Nordskog
10. 1959
11. Hazel
12. 1943
13. Variances and covariances
14. Second order
15. Two
16. Six
17. Selection indices
18. 100%
19. Maize
20. Brim *et al.*

TRUE OR FALSE

1. False	2. True	3. False
4. False	5. True	6. True
7. True	8. True	9. False
10. True	11. False	12. True
13. True	14. True	15. True
16. True	17. True	18. False
19. False	20. True	

APPROPRIATE TERM

1. Discriminant function
2. Selection index
3. Classical selection index
4. Restricted selection index
5. General selection index
6. Weight coefficient
7. Relative efficiency
8. GS_1
9. GS_2

●●●

7

CHAPTER

Diallel Mating Design

A. DEFINITIONS

Diallel cross. Mating of selected genotypes in all possible combinations *i.e.*, $n(n-1)/2$ among n parents. It is of two types, *viz.* half diallel and full diallel.

Half diallel. All possible one way (direct) crosses among n genotypes *i.e.* $n(n-1)/2$.

Full diallel. All possible both way (direct and reciprocal) crosses among n genotype *i.e.* $n(n-1)$.

Diallel analysis. Evaluation of a set of diallel crosses.

Complete diallel. All possible single crosses *i.e.* $n(n-1)/2$ among n parents.

Vr-Wr graph. A graph which is constructed in the Hayman's approach of diallel analysis.

Fixed effect model. A method of diallel analysis which is used with diallel set of crosses made among fixed sample of inbred lines. It provides information about individual line.

Random effect model. A method of diallel analysis which is used with diallel set of crosses made among random samples of individuals from random mating population. It provides information about population as a whole.

Array. A group of crosses, in a diallel set, in which a particular parent is common.

Degree of dominance. The ratio of dominance variance of additive variance.

B. BACKGROUND INFORMATION

1. The term diallel was coined by Yates (1947).
2. The graphical approach of diallel analysis was initially developed by Jinks and Hayman in 1953.
3. The numerical approach of diallel analysis was developed by Griffing (1956).
4. In diallel cross each parent has equal chance to mate with every other parent.

5. Graphical approach involves Vr-Wr graph.
6. Graphical approach provides information about six components, *viz.* D, H_1, H_2, E, F and h^2.
7. In Vr-Wr graph when regression line passes through the origin, it indicates complete dominance.
8. When the regression line passes above the origin cutting Wr-axis, it indicates partial dominance.
9. In Vr-Wr graph, when the regression line passes above the origin cutting Wr-axis and touching the limiting parabola, it reveals absence of dominance.
10. When the regression line passes below the origin cutting the Vr-axis, it indicates the presence of overdominance.
11. In Vr-Wr graph, parents with more dominant genes are located nearer to the origin.
12. In Vr-Wr graph, parents with more recessive genes fall farther from the origin.
13. In Vr-Wr graph, parents with equal frequencies of dominant and recessive genes occupy intermediate position.
14. Griffing (1956) provides four methods of estimating combining ability from a diallel cross.
15. Numerical approach of diallel analysis provides information about D and H components through gca and sca variances and effects.
16. In Griffing's approach, calculation of genetic ratios is not possible.
17. In Griffing's analysis of diallel cross, the additive genetic variance is equal to twice gca variance.
18. In Griffing's approach of diallel analysis, the dominance variance is equal to sca variance.
19. Fixed effect model of combining ability analysis of diallel cross provides information about individual line.
20. Random effect model of combining analysis of diallel cross provides information about the parent population as a whole.
21. Griffing's analysis of diallel cross provides information about gca and sca variances and effects.
22. In 1956, Jinks provided the procedure for graphical analysis of dialel cross from F_2 data.
23. The total number of crosses among n parents in a half diallel is equal to $n(n-1)/2$.
24. In full diallel, the total number of crosses among n parents is equal to $n(n-1)$.
25. Half diallel does not permit estimation of maternal effects.
26. Full diallel permits estimation of maternal effects.
27. In full diallel, each parent is used as male and female in the mating.
28. In half diallel, each parent is used either as male or female in the mating.
29. Half diallel can be used even when some parents have male sterlity or self incompatibility.
30. Full diallel can be used only when parents donot have female sterility.

31. The diallel analysis in self pollinated species was first carried out by Jinks (1954) and Hayman (1954).
32. Diallel analysis is based on seven genetical assumptions, *viz*. (1) normal diploid segregation, (2) lack of maternal effects, (3) absense of multiple alleles, (4) homozygosity of parents, (5) absence of linkage, (6) absence of epistasis, and (7) random mating.
33. Seven assumptions for the analysis of diallel cross were proposed by Hayman (1954).
34. Griffing's method 1 of diallel analysis includes parents, direct crosses and reciprocal crosses in the analysis.
35. Griffing's method 2 of diallel analysis involves one way (direct) crosses and parents in the analysis.
36. Griffing's method 3 of diallel analysis includes direct and reciprocal crosses in the analysis.
37. In diallel cross, average degree of dominance is estimated as $\sqrt{H_1/D}$.
38. The number of gene groups which control the character and exhibit dominance is estimated as h^2/H_2.
39. The proportion of genes with positive and negative effects in the parents is estimated as $H_2/4H_1$.

C. MULTIPLE CHOICE

1. The term diallel was coined in 1947 by :
   (a) Yates (b) Hayman
   (c) Griffing (d) Kempthorne.
2. Yates coined the term diallel in :
   (a) 1953 (b) 1954
   (c) 1947 (d) 1956.
3. In 1953, who proposed the graphical approach of diallel analysis :
   (a) Mather and Jinks (b) Jinks and Hayman
   (c) Jinks and Jones (d) None of these.
4. Jinks and Hayman proposed the graphical approach of diallel analysis in :
   (a) 1947 (b) 1953
   (c) 1954 (d) 1957.
5. Who proposed the numerical approach of diallel analysis in 1956 :
   (a) Mather (b) Hayman
   (c) Griffing (d) Falconer
6. Griffing proposed the numerical approach of diallel cross analysis in :
   (a) 1947 (b) 1953
   (c) 1956 (d) 1957.
7. In a half diallel, total number of crosses among n parents would be :
   (a) $n(n - 1)/2$ (b) $n(n + 1)/2$
   (c) $n(n - 1)$ (d) $n(n + 1)$.

8. How many entries would be there for evaluation in a 8 × 8 half diallel including parents ?
   (a) 56 (b) 36
   (c) 28 (d) 64.

9. How many entries including parents are there in 10 × 10 full diallel cross ?
   (a) 45 (b) 55
   (c) 90 (d) 100.

10. In a diallel cross, n^2 combinations among n parents include :
    (a) Direct crosses (b) Reciprocal crosses
    (c) Parents (d) All of these.

11. Graphical approach of diallel analysis provides information about :
    (a) D and H_1 (b) H_2 and E
    (c) F and h^2 (d) All of these.

12. How many components can be obtained by graphical approach of diallel analysis ?
    (a) Two (b) Four
    (c) Five (d) Six.

13. Numerical approach of diallel analysis provides information about :
    (a) D and H components (b) gca and sca variances
    (c) gca and sca effects (d) All of these.

14. In diallel analysis, the dominance variance is equal to :
    (a) sca variance (b) 2 v-sca
    (c) 2 v-gca (d) None of these.

15. In diallel analysis, the additive genetic variance is equal to :
    (a) 2v sca (b) 2v gca
    (c) v sca (d) v gca.

16. In 1956, the procedure of graphical analysis of diallel cross from F_2 data was provided by :
    (a) Hayman (b) Jinks
    (c) Griffing (d) Kempthorne.

17. Jinks provided the procedure of graphical analysis of diallel analysis from F_2 data in :
    (a) 1947 (b) 1953
    (c) 1954 (d) 1956.

18. How many genetical assumptions are involved in diallel analysis :
    (a) Three (b) Four
    (c) Six (d) Seven.

19. For diallel analysis seven genetical assumptions were proposed in 1954 by :
    (a) Yates (b) Smith
    (c) Hayman (d) Griffing.

20. Hayman proposed seven genetical assumptions for diallel analysis in :
    (a) 1947 (b) 1953
    (c) 1954 (d) 1956.

21. Half diallel does not permit estimation of :

(a) gca effects (b) sca effects
(c) Maternal effects (d) All of these.

22. Full diallel permits estimation of :

(a) gca and sca effects (b) Maternal effects
(c) gca and sca variances (d) All of these.

23. How many methods of diallel analysis have been given by Griffing (1956) :

(a) One (b) Two
(c) Three (d) Four.

24. Griffing's method one of diallel analysis involves :

(a) Parents (b) Direct crosses
(c) Reciprocal crosses (d) All of these.

25. In Vr-Wr graph when regression line passes through the origin, it indicates :

(a) Complete dominance (b) Partial dominance
(c) Lack of dominance (d) Overdominance.

26. In Vr-Wr graph, parents with more dominant genes occupy position :

(a) Near origin (b) Far away from origin
(c) In the middle (d) All of these.

27. Diallel cross does not permit estimation of :

(a) Additive variance (b) Dominance variance
(c) Epistatic variance (d) All of these.

28. In diallel cross, average degree of dominance is estimated as :

(a) $\sqrt{H_1/D}$ (b) h^2/H_2
(c) $H_2/4H1$ (d) None of these.

29. In diallel cross, the proportion of genes with positive and negative effects in the parents is estimated as :

(a) h^2/H_2 (b) $\sqrt{H_1/D}$
(c) $H_2/4H_1$ (d) D/H_1.

30. Yates coined the term :

(a) Diallel cross (b) Partial dialles
(c) Line × tester (d) Triple test cross.

D. FILL IN THE BLANKS

1. The term diallel was coined by ....
2. The term diallel was coined by Yates in ....
3. Graphical approach of diallel analysis was proposed by ....
4. Numerical approach of diallel analysis was given by ....
5. A diallel with F_1s and parents is known as ....
6. A diallel with F_1s and reciprocals is referred to as ....

7. With n parents, total number of crosses in a full diallel is equal to ....
8. With n parents, total number of crosses in a half diallel is equal to ....
9. A graph constructed in a diallel cross is called ....
10. In self-pollinated species, diallel analysis was first used by ....
11. Graphical approach of diallel analysis provides information about .... components.
12. In diallel analysis, the dominance genetic variance is equal to ....
13. In diallell cross, the additive genetic variance is equal to ....
14. The procedure of diallel analysis from F_2 data was outlined by ....
15. Diallel analysis is based on .... genetical assumptions.
16. Seven genetical assumptions for diallel analysis were proposed by ....
17. Half diallel does not permit estimation of .... effects.
18. In Vr-Wr graph, when regression line passes through the origin, it indicates ....
19. Griffing provided .... methods of diallel analysis.
20. A graph which is constructed in the Hayman's approach of diallel analysis is called ....
21. The ratio of dominance variance to additive variance is called ....
22. Evaluation of a set of diallel crosses is called ....
23. Diallel cross fails to provide estimates of .... variance.
24. In a diallel cross, average degree of dominance is estimated as ....
25. The proportion of genes with positive and genetive effects in the parents is estimated as ....

E. MARK TRUE OR FALSE

1. The term diallel was coined by Hayman (1954).
2. Numerical approach of diallel analysis was proposed by Griffing (1956).
3. Graphical approach of diallel cross analysis was proposed by Hayman (1954).
4. In half dialled, total number of crosses among n parents is equal to $n(n - 1)$.
5. In full diallel, total number of crosses among n parents is equal to $n(n - 1)/2$.
6. In half diallel, each parent is used either as male or female in crossing programme.
7. In full diallel, each parent is used both as male and female in the crossing programme.
8. Numerical approach of diallel analysis is based on the estimates of combining ability effects and variances.
9. Vr-Wr graph is constructed in Griffing's approach of diallel analysis.
10. Diallel cross provides information about additive and dominance variances.
11. Diallel cross fails to provide estimate of epistatic variance.
12. In diallel cross, each parent has equal chance to mate with every other parent.
13. Half diallel permits estimation of maternal effects.

14. Full diallel does not permit estimation of maternal effects.
15. Random effect model of combining ability analysis is used with a set of inbred lines or fixed varieties.
16. Fixed effect model of combining ability analysis is used with random mating population.
17. Diallel analysis is based an seven genetical assumptions.
18. Seven generical assumptions for diallel analysis were proposed by Griffing (1956).
19. In Vr-Wr graph, parents with more dominant genes are located near the origin.
20. On Vr-Wr graph, parents with more recessive genes occupy intermediate position.
21. On Vr-Wr graph, parents with equal frequencies of dominant and recessive genes are located far away from the origin.
22. When the regression line passes through the origin it indicated lack of dominance.
23. When the regression line passes above the origin, cutting Wr-axis, it indicates partial dominance.
24. When the regression line passes above the origin cutting Wr-axis and touching limiting parabola, it indicates overdominance.
25. When the regression lines passes below the origin cutting Vr-axis, it indicates complete dominance.
26. Method 1 of diallel analysis includes F_1 one-way crosses only.
27. Method 2 of diallel cross involves direct crosses and parents in the analysis.
28. Method 3 of diallel cross involves direct and reciprocal crosses in the analysis.
29. Method 4 of diallel cross involves parents, direct cross and reciprocals in the analysis.
30. The proportion of genes with positive and negative effects in the parents is estimated as $H_2/4H_1$.

F. USE APPROPRIATE TERM

1. Mating of selected parents in all possible combinations.
2. All possible one way (direct) crosses among *n* parents.
3. All possible both ways (direct and reciprocal) crosses among *n* parents.
4. Evaluation of a set of diallel crosses.
5. A graph which is constructed in the Hayman's approach of diallel analysis.
6. A method of analysis of diallel set used with fixed sample of inbred lines.
7. A method of diallel analysis used with crosses made among individuals of random mating population.
8. The ratio of dominance variance to additive variance.

ANSWERS

MULTIPLE CHOICE

1. (a) Yates
2. (c) 1947
3. (b) Jinks and Hayman
4. (b) 1953
5. (c) Griffing
6. (c) 1956
7. (a) $n(n - 1)/2$

8. (b) 36
9. (d) 100
10. (d) All of these
11. (d) All of these
12. (d) Six
13. (d) All of these
14. (a) sca variance
15. (b) 2v gca
16. (b) Jinks
17. (d) 1956
18. (d) Seven
19. (c) Hayman
20. (c) 1954
21. (c) Maternal-effects
22. (d) All of these
23. (d) Four
24. (d) All of these
25. (a) Complete dominance
26. (a) Near origin
27. (c) Epistatic variance
28. (a) $\sqrt{H_1/D}$
29. (c) $H_2/4H_1$
30. (a) Diallel cross

FILL IN THE BLANKS

1. Yates
2. 1947
3. Jinks and Hayman
4. Griffing
5. Half diallel
6. Full diallel
7. $n(n-1)$
8. $n(n-1)/2$
9. Vr-Wr graph
10. Hayman
11. Six (D_1, H_1, H_2, E, F, h^2)
12. v sca
13. 2v gca
14. Jinks
15. Seven
16. Hayman
17. Maternal
18. Complete dominance
19. Four
20. Vr-Wr graph
21. Degree of dominance
22. Dialled analysis
23. Epistatic
24. $\sqrt{H_1/D}$
25. $H_2/4H_1$

TRUE OR FALSE

1. False	2. True	3. True
4. False	5. False	6. True
7. True	8. True	9. False
10. True	11. True	12. True
13. False	14. False	15. False
16. False	17. True	18. False
19. True	20. False	21. False
22. False	23. True	24. False
25. False	26. False	27. True
28. True	29. False	30. True

APPROPRIATE TERM

1. Diallel
2. Half diallel
3. Full diallel
4. Diallel analysis
5. Vr-Wr graph
6. Fixed effect model
7. Random-effect model
8. Degree of dominance

●●●

8

CHAPTER

Partial Diallel and Line × Tester Techniques

A. DEFINITIONS

Partial diallel. A modified form of a diallel cross in which only a part of all possible crosses from diallel mating is used for analysis; also called fractional diallel cross or incomplete diallel.

Fractional diallel. Same as partial diallel.

Incomplete diallel. Same as partial diallel.

Full sib. Progeny of the mating of two individuals.

Half sib. Progeny having one parent in common.

Tester. A common parent used in crossing with several lines.

Top crosses. Various crosses made using a common tester; also called test crosses.

Test crosses. Same as top crosses.

Line × Tester cross. A modified form of top cross which is used for measuring general and specific combining ability variances and effects in large number of germplasm lines at a time.

B. BACKGROUND INFORMATION

1. The concept of partial diallel mating design was developed by Kempthorne in 1957.
2. In 1961, the partial diallel was further elaborated by Kempthorne and Curnow.
3. Partial diallel utilizes only a part of all possible crosses form a diallel cross.
4. In partial diallel, each parent is crossed to some of the other parents, but not all.
5. In partial diallel, total number of crosses is equal to $ns/2$, where n is number of parents and s in the number of sample crosses.

6. Partial diallel provides information about gca and sca variances and gca effects.
7. Partial diallel also provides information about D and H components.
8. Partial diallel does not provide information about sca effects.
9. Partial diallel permits evaluation of more inbred lines at a time than by a complete diallel cross.
10. Results obtained from partial diallel have lesser precision than those obtained by diallel analysis.
11. The n should be a whole number. It can not be in decimal fraction.
12. The s (number of sample crosses) should be either greater than or equal to $n/2$.
13. Both n and s can neither be odd nor even. If n is odd s should be even and *vice versa*.
14. A constant $k = (n + 1 - s)/2$, where n and s are number of parents and sample crosses, respectively.
15. In partial diallel, graphical approach of analysis is not applicable.
16. In partial diallel, there is only one method of estimating combining ability variences and effects.
17. Partial diallel is only of one type.
18. In partial diallel, reciprocal crosses are not used for analysis.
19. In partial diallel, additive guretic variance is equal to twice gca variance (2vgca).
20. The dominance variance is equal to sca variance (Vsca).
21. The concept of line × tester cross analysis was developed by Kempthorne in 1957.
22. In line × tester technique, total number of crosses is equal of mf, where m and f are number of male and female parents, respectively.
23. In line × tester design, each male is mated to each female, but there is no intermating among the males and among females.
24. In line × tester design, each male is crossed to the same set of females.
25. Line × tester design, provides information about gca and sca variances and effects and also about D and H components.
26. Line × tester design, permits evaluation of larger number of lines than diallel and partial diallel crosses.
27. In line × tester cross, additive genetic variance is equal to gca variance.
28. In line × tester cross, dominance variance is equal to sca variance.
29. Line × tester analysis does not involve graphical approach.
30. In line × tester cross, each parent does not get equal chance to mate with every other parent.
31. Line × tester analysis has only one method of analysis.
32. Line × tester cross does not involve reciprocal crosses in the analysis.

C. MULTIPLE CHOICE

1. The concept of partial diallel was proposed in 1957 by :
   (a) Yates (b) Hayman
   (c) Griffing (d) Kempthorne.
2. Kempthorne developed the concept of partial diallel in :
   (a) 1947 (b) 1954
   (c) 1956 (d) 1957.
3. Partial diallel is also known as :
   (a) Fractional diallel (b) Incomplete diallel
   (c) (a) and (b) (d) None of these.
4. Partial diallel was further elaborated in 1961 by :
   (a) Mather and Jinks (b) Kempthorne and Curnow
   (c) Jinkes and Jones (d) None of these.
5. Kempthorne and Curnow further elaborated the concept of partial diallel in :
   (a) 1947 (b) 1953
   (c) 1954 (d) 1961.
6. Partial diallel utilizes only a part from diallel crosses of :
   (a) Direct crosses (b) Reciprocal crosses
   (c) Both (a) and (b) (d) None of these.
7. In partial diallel, each parent has chance to mate with :
   (a) All other parents (b) Few other parents
   (c) A common set of parents (d) None of these.
8. In partial diallel, total number of crosses is equal to :
   (a) $n(n - 1)/2$ (b) $ns/2$
   (c) n^2 (d) $n(n + 1)$.
9. Partial diallel provides information about :
   (a) gca variance (b) sca variance
   (c) gca effects (d) All of these.
10. Partial diallel does not provides information about :
    (a) Additive variance (b) Dominant variance
    (c) gca effect (d) sca effect.
11. In partial diallel what should be the s (number of sample crosses) using n parents ?
    (a) N/2 (b) $n/3$
    (c) $n/4$ (d) All of these.
12. Which of the following is not related to partial diallel ?
    (a) D and H components (b) gca variance
    (c) sca variance (d) Vr-Wr graph.
13. In partial diallel, additive genetic variance is equal to :
    (a) gca variance (b) Twice gca variance
    (c) sca variance (d) None of these.

14. In partial diallel, dominance variance is equal to :

(a) sca variance (b) Twice sca variance
(c) gca variance (d) All of these.

15. With n = 20 and s = 11 how many crosses have to be made in a partial diallel ?

(a) 220 (b) 110
(c) 190 (d) None of these.

16. Which of the following formulae is used for estimating a constant (k) in partial diallel cross ?

(a) $n(n - 1)/2$ (b) $n(n + 1)/2$
(c) $n(n + 1 - s)/2$ (d) None of these.

17. In partial diallel, how many methods of combining ability analysis are available ?

(a) One (b) Two
(c) Three (d) Four.

18. Which of the following scientists is associated with partial diallel ?

(a) Hayman (b) Griffing
(c) Kempthorne (d) Anderson.

19. Who developed the concept of line × tester cross analysis ?

(a) Kempthorne (b) Jinks
(c) Jinks and Jones (d) Mather.

20. Kempthorne proposed line × tester cross analysis in :

(a) 1953 (b) 1954
(c) 1956 (d) 1957.

21. In line × tester cross, each male is mated with :

(a) Same set of females (b) Different set of females
(c) Few females of a set (d) All of these.

22. In line × tester cross mating is done between :

(a) Males and females (b) Among males
(c) Among females (d) All of these.

23. Line × tester analysis does not permit mating between :

(a) Males and femals (b) Among males
(c) Among females (d) (b) and (c) above.

24. Line × tester analysis provides information about :

(a) gca and sca variances (b) gca and sca effects
(c) D and H components (d) All of these.

25. In line × tester analysis, additive genetic variance is equal to :

(a) gca variance (b) 2 gca variance
(c) $\sqrt{v\, gca}$ (d) v gca/2.

26. In line × tester analysis, dominance variance is equal to :

(a) $\sqrt{sca\text{ variance}}$ (b) ½ sca variance
(c) sca variance (d) None of these.

27. Line × tester cross is a modified form of :

(a) Top cross (b) Polycross
(c) Back cross (d) None of these.

28. Maximum number of parents can be evaluated for combining ability at a time by :

(a) Diallel cross (b) Partial diallel cross
(c) Linc × tester cross (d) Polycross

29. A good tester should possess :

(a) Brood genetic bose (b) Wider adaptability
(c) Low yield potential (d) All of these.

D. FILL IN THE BLANKS

1. The concept of partial diallel was developed by ....
2. Kempthorne developed the concept of partial diallel in ....
3. Partial diallel was further elaborated by ....
4. Partial diallel is also known as ....
5. Incomplete diallel refers to ....
6. Partial diallel fails to provide information about .... effects.
7. In partial diallel, total crosses are equal to ....
8. In partial diallel, additive variance is equal to ....
9. In partial diallel, dominance variance is equal to ....
10. In partial diallel the formula .... is used to find out the value of constant k.
11. The concept of line × tester cross was developed by............
12. Kempthorne developed the concept of line × tester analysis in ....
13. Line × tester cross is a modified form of ....
14. In line × tester analysis the common male parents are called ....
15. In line × tester cross female parents are called ....
16. Kempthorne was professor of .... at Iowa State College USA
17. Kempthorne was native of ....
18. The famous book "Introduction to Genetic Statistics was written by ....
19. The book Introduction to Genetic Statistics was first published in ....
20. In line × tester cross, additive variance is equal to ....
21. In line × tester cross, dominance variances is equal to ....
22. Using 10 parents, total crosses in a partial diallel would be ....

E. MARK TRUE OR FALSE

1. Hayman developed the concept of partial diallel.
2. Partiallel diallel is also called fractional diallel.
3. The concept of partial diallel was developed in 1950.
4. Partial diallel provides information about sca effects.

5. In partial diallel, if the n is odd s should be even.
6. In partial diallel, if the n is odd s should be even.
7. In partial diallel, a constant k is estimated as $(n + 1 - s)/2$.
8. Graphical approach is not used in partial diallel.
9. Reciprocal crosses are not used in partial diallel.
10. In partial diallel, each parent is crossed to all other parents.
11. Partial diallel utilizes one part of all possible crosses from a diallel cross.
12. In partial diallel, dominance variance is equal to 2 v sca.
13. Kempthorne developed the concept of line × tester cross in 1957.
14. In line × tester cross each male is crossed to the different set of females.
15. In line × tester cross, intermating is also done among males and among females.
16. In line × tester cross, additive variance is equal to gca variance.
17. In line × tester cross, each parent is crossed to every other parent.
18. In Line × tester cross, graphical approach is used.
19. In partial diallel, additive variance is equal to twice gca variance.
20. Kemptherne is native of England.
21. The book Introduction to Genetic Statistics was written by Kempthorne.
22. Kempthorne was professor of physics at Iowa State College USA.

F. USE APPROPRIATE TERM

1. A modified form of a diallel cross in which only a part of all possible crosses from diallel mating is used for analysis.
2. Progeny of the mating of two individuals.
3. Progeny having one parent in common.
4. A common parent used in crossing with several lines.
5. Various crosses made using a common tester.
6. A modified form of top cross involving some parents as females and others as males.

ANSWERS

MULTIPLE CHOICE

1. (d) Kempthorne
2. (d) 1957
3. (c) (a) and (b)
4. (b) Kempthorne and Curnow
5. (d) 1961
6. (a) Direct crosses
7. (b) Few other parents
8. (b) $ns/2$
9. (d) All of these
10. (d) sca effects
11. (a) $n/2$
12. (d) Vr-Wr graph
13. (b) 2 v gca
14. (a) sca variance
15. (b) 110
16. (c) $(n + 1 - s)/2$
17. (a) One
18. (c) Kempthorne
19. (a) Kampthorne

20. (d) 1957
21. (c) Same set of females
22. (a) Male and females
23. (d) (b) and (c) above
24. (d) All of these
25. (a) gca variance
26. (c) sca variance
27. (a) Top cross
28. (c) Line × tester cross
29. (d) All of these

FILL IN THE BLANKS

1. Kempthorne
2. 1957
3. Kempthorne and Curnow
4. Fractional diallel
5. Partial diallel
6. sca effects
7. ns/2
8. 2 v gca
9. v sca
10. $(n + 1 - s)/2$
11. Kempthorne
12. 1957
13. Top cross
14. Testers
15. Lines
16. Statistics
17. USA
18. Kempthorne
19. 1957
20. v gca
21. v sca
22. 25

TRUE OR FALSE

1. False	**2.** True	**3.** False
4. False	**5.** True	**6.** True
7. True	**8.** True	**9.** True
10. False	**11.** True	**12.** False
13. True	**14.** False	**15.** False
16. True	**17.** False	**18.** False
19. True	**20.** False	**21.** True
22. False		

APPROPRIATE TERM

1. Partial diallel
2. Full sib
3. Half sib
4. Tester
5. Top crosses
6. Line × tester cross

●●●

9

CHAPTER

Triallel and Quadriallel Analysis

A. DEFINITIONS

Three-way Cross. A cross involving three different parents. In other words, it is a cross between F_1 hybrid and an inbred line/pure line.

Triallel Cross. Same as three way cross.

Triallel Analysis. Analysis of all possible three way crosses among n parents (selected parents).

Double Cross. A cross involving four different parents. In other words, it is a cross between two single F_1 crosses *i.e.,* (A × B) × (C × D).

Quadriallel Cross. Same as double cross.

Quadriallel Analysis. Analysis of all possible double crosses among n (selected) parents.

B. BACKGROUND INFORMATION

1. The concept of triallel cross analysis was developed by Rawlings and Cokerham (1962a).
2. Triallel analysis includes all possible three way crosses among n parents.
3. Triallel analysis refers to analysis of three way crosses.
4. In triallel analysis, total number of three way crosses among n parents is equal to $n(n - 1)(n - 2)/2$.
5. In triallel, each parent involves three different parents.
6. Triallel cross provides information about addition (D), dominance (H) and epistitic components.

7. Three way crosses are made in such a way that no parent should appear more than once in the same three way cross.
8. Triallel analysis helps in deciding the mating order of parents for developing superior three way hybrids and obtaining superior recombinants/segregants.
9. In triallel, more crosses than diallel have to be made using same number of parents.
10. The variance components in a series of three way crosses is equal to

$$\frac{3}{4}\text{VA} + \frac{1}{2}\text{VD} + \frac{9}{16}\text{VAA} + \frac{3}{8}\text{VAD} + \frac{1}{4}\text{VDD} + \ldots$$

11. For analysis, three way crosses require three crop seasons, two crop seasons for generating material and third season for evaluation.
12. It helps in estimation of general line effects (first and second kind), specific line effects (two line specific effect of first kind, two lines specific line effect of second kind) and three line specific effect.
13. The lines which are used in single cross are known as grand parents.
14. The lines which are crossed with single cross to obtain three way crosses are called parents.
15. General line effect of first kind refers to the general combining ability effect of a line used as one of the grand parents.
16. General line effect of second order refers to the gca effect of a line used as parent crossed to the single cross hybrid.
17. Two line specific effect of first kind refers to the sca effect of a line used as one of the grand parents.
18. Two line specific effect of second kind refers to the sca effect of a line crossed to the single cross hybrid as a parent.
19. Three line specific effect refers to sca effect of a line in three way cross.
20. The performance of three way cross is predicted from the average performance of two non parental single crosses.
21. The performance of a three way cross say $(P_1 \times P_2) \times P_3$ would be predicted as $[(P_1 \times P_3) + (P_2 \times P_3)]/2$.
22. The concept of quadriallel cross analysis was developed by Rawlings and Cokerham (1962b).
23. Quadriallel analysis involves all possible double crosses among n parents.
24. Quadriallel analysis refers to analysis of double crosses made in a diallel fashion.
25. In quadriallel cross, each cross involves four different parents.
26. In quadriallel analysis, total number of double crosses among n parents is equal to $n(n-1)(n-2)(n-3)/8$.
27. Quadriallel cross provides information about additive, dominance and epistatic variances.
28. Double crosses are made in diallel fashion among F_1 crosses in such a way that no parent should appear more than once in the same double cross.
29. Quadriallel analysis provides information about the order in which parents should be crossed to develop productive double cross and obtain superior segregants.

30. In quadriallel analysis, more crosses than diallel and triallel have to be made *i.e.* 630 crosses among 10 parents.

31. The variance components in a serious of double crosses is equal to

$$\tfrac{1}{2}\text{VA} + \tfrac{1}{4}\text{VD} + \tfrac{1}{4}\text{VAA} + \tfrac{1}{8}\text{VAD} + \tfrac{1}{16}\text{VDD} + \ldots$$

32. In quadriallel analysis, sca effects are estimated as interactions involving two lines, three lines and four lines.

33. Quadriallel analysis, provides information about one, two, three and four lines average effects.

(i) one line average effects represent primarily additive gene action.

(ii) two lines average effects represent non additive gene action.

(iii) three line average effects represent additive × dominance interaction including all three factor or higher order interactions except all dominant types.

(iv) four line average effects represent dominance × dominance interaction and all three factor interactions, except all additive types.

34. A method for predicting the performance of double cross hybrid was given by Jenkins (1934).

35. The performance of a double cross hybrid is predicted from the average performance of non-parental single crosses.

Performance of double cross say

$$(P_1 \times P_2) \times (P_3 \times P_4) = \frac{(P_1 \times P_3) + (P_1 \times P_4) + (P_2 \times P_3) + (P_2 \times P_4)}{4}$$

36. More gain is expected through selection in single crosses than in three way crosses and double crosses in maize.

C. MULTIPLE CHOICE

1. The concept of triallel analysis was developed in 1962 by :

(a) Mather and Jinks (b) Jinks and Hayman
(c) Rawlings and Cokerham (d) None of these.

2. Rawlings and Cokerham developed the concept of triallel analysis in :

(a) 1953 (b) 1956
(c) 1962 (d) 1981.

3. Triallel cross refers to :

(a) Three way crosses (b) Single crosses
(c) Double crosses (d) Multiple crosses.

4. In triallel, total number of crosses is equal to :

(a) $n(n-1)/2$ (b) $n(n+1)/2$
(c) $n(n-1)(n-2)/2$ (d) None of these.

5. How many crop seasons are required for triallel analysis ?

(a) One (b) Two
(c) Three (d) Four.

6. In triallel cross, each parent appears :
(a) Once (b) Twice
(c) Thrice (d) Four times.

7. How many parents are involved in each triallel cross ?
(a) One (b) Two
(c) Three (d) Four.

8. Triallel and quadriallel analysis provide information about :
(a) Additive variance (b) Dominance variance
(c) Epistatic variance (d) All of these.

9. Using 10 parents in which of the following designs maximum crosses have to be effected ?
(a) Diallel cross (b) Partial diallel
(c) Triallel cross (d) Quadriallel cross.

10. Using 10 parents in which of the following designs minimum crosses have to be effected ?
(a) Partial diallel (b) Diallel
(c) Triallel (d) Quadriallel.

11. For triallel analysis, crosses are effected in which of the following ways ?
(a) Diallel fashion (b) Partial diallel fashion
(c) Line × tester fashion (d) None of these.

12. Triallel analysis estimates general line effects of :
(a) First kind (b) Second kind
(c) (a) and (b) (d) Third kind.

13. Triallel analysis provides information about two line specific effects of :
(a) First kind (b) Second kind
(c) (a) and (b) (d) None of these.

14. Which of the following provides information for deciding mating order of parents to obtain superior double cross ?
(a) Diallel cross (b) Partial diallel cross
(c) Triallel cross (d) Quadriallel cross.

15. Who developed the concept of quadriallel cross ?
(a) Rawlings and Cokerham (b) Mather and Jinks
(c) Jinks and Jones (d) None of these.

16. The concept of quadriallel cross was developed by Rawlings and Cokerham in :
(a) 1953 (b) 1954
(c) 1962 (d) 1975.

17. How many crop seasons are required for quadriallel analysis ?
(a) One (b) Two
(c) Three (d) Four.

18. In which of the following fashion quadriallel crosses are made ?
(a) Diallel (b) Partial diallel
(c) Line × tester (d) None of these.

19. Using 10 parents, how many quadriallel crosses have to be made ?
(a) 25 (b) 45
(c) 360 (d) 630.

20. In quadriallel analysis, total number of crosses is equal to :
(a) $n(n-1)/2$ (b) $n_3/2$
(c) $n(n-1)(n-2)/2$ (d) $n(n-1)(n-2)(n-3)/8$.

21. How many parents are involved in each quadriallel cross :
(a) Two (b) Three
(c) Four (d) Five.

22. In quadriallel analysis, sca effects are estimated as interactions involving :
(a) Two lines (b) Three lines
(c) Four lines (d) All of these.

23. In quadriallel analysis, one line average effects represent :
(a) Additive gene action (b) Dominance gene action
(c) Epistatic gene action (d) All of these.

24. The method for predicting the performance of double cross hybrid was given in 1934 by :
(a) Mather (b) Jenkins
(c) Hayman (d) Jinks.

25. Jenkins provided method for predicting the performance of double cross hybrid in :
(a) 1921 (b) 1934
(c) 1954 (d) 1962.

26. In which of the following populations of maize maximum gain is expected through selection ?
(a) Single crosses (b) Three way crosses
(c) Double crosses (d) Multiple crosses.

D. FILL IN THE BLANKS

1. The concept of triallel cross analysis was developed by ....

2. Rawlings and Cokerham coined the term triallel cross in ....

3. Triallel cross refers to ....

4. In triallel analysis, total number of crosses among n parents is equal to ....

5. Triallel crosses are made in .... fashion.

6. Triallel analysis requires .... Crop seasons.

7. In triallel analysis, lines which are used in single cross are called ....

8. Lines which are used for crossing with single crosses are known as ....

9. The gca effect of a line used as grand parent is called general line effect of ....

10. The gca effect of a line used as parent is known as general line effect of ....

11. The sca effect of a line used as grand parent is called two line specific effect of ....

12. The sca effect of line used as parent is called two line specific effect of ....

13. The concept of quadriallel analysis was developed by ....
14. Rawlings and Cokerham developed the concept of quadriallel analysis in ....
15. Total number of quadriallel crosses among on parents is equal to ....
16. Triallel analysis refers to ....
17. Quadriallel crosses are made in .... fashion.
18. Quadriallel analysis requires .... crop seasons.
19. A method for predicting the performance of double cross was given by ....
20. Performance of a double cross hybrid is predicted from the average performance of .... single crosses.

E. MARK TRUE OR FALSE

1. The concept of triallel cross analysis was developed by Hayman.
2. Triallel crosses are made in line × tester fashion.
3. Each triallel cross involves three parents.
4. Triallel cross is also called three way cross.
5. Total triallel crosses among n parents are equal to $n(n - 1)(n + 1)/2$.
6. Three way cross analysis requires two crop seasons.
7. Three way crosses are made on such a way than no parent should appear more than once in the same three way cross.
8. In triallel cross, lines which are used to make single cross are called parents.
9. Lines which are crossed with single cross are called grand parents.
10. The performance of three way cross $(P_1 \times P_2) \times P_3$ is predicted as $[(P_1 \times P_3) + (P_2 \times P_3)]/2$.
11. Triallel and quadriallel analysis do not provide information about epistatic variance.
12. The concept of quadriallel analysis was developed by Jinks.
13. Quadriallel cross refers to double cross.
14. The number of quadriallel crosses among n parents is equal to $n(n - 1)(n - 2)(n - 3)/8$.
15. In quadriallel analysis, each cross involves three parents.
16. Quadriallel crosses are made in a diallel fashion.
17. In quadriallel analysis more crosses than diallel and triallel using same number of parents have to be made.
18. Quadriallel analysis is useful to decide order of crossing parents to obtain productive double cross hybrids.
19. Jenkins provided a method for predicting performance of double cross hybrid.
20. The average performance of four non-potential single crosses is used to predict the performance of a double cross.

F. USE APPROPRIATE TERM

1. A cross involving three different parents.
2. Analysis of all possible three way crosses among n parents.
3. A cross involving four different parents.
4. Analysis of all possible double crosses among n parents.

ANSWERS

MULTIPLE CHOICE

1. (c) Rawlings and Cokerham
2. (c) 1962
3. (a) Three way cross
4. (c) $n(n-1)(n-2)/2$
5. (c) Three
6. (a) Once
7. (c) Three
8. (d) All of these
9. (d) Quadriallel cross
10. (b) Diallel
11. (a) Diallel fashion
12. (c) (a) and (b)
13. (c) (a) and (b)
14. (c) Triallel cross
15. (a) Rawlings and Cokerham
16. (c) 1962
17. (c) Three
18. (a) Diallel
19. (d) 630
20. (d) $n(n-1)(n-2)(n-3)/8$
21. (c) Four
22. (d) All of these
23. (a) Additive gene action
24. (b) Jenkins
25. (b) 1934
26. (a) Single crosses

FILL IN THE BLANKS

1. Rawlings and Cokerham
2. 1962
3. Three way cross
4. $n(n-1)(n-2)/2$
5. Diallel
6. Three
7. Grand parents
8. Parents
9. First kind
10. Second kind
11. First kind
12. Second kind
13. Rawlings and Cokerham
14. 1962
15. $n(n-1)(n-2)(n-3)/8$
16. Double cross analysis
17. Diallel
18. Three
19. Jenkins
20. Non parental

TRUE OR FALSE

1. False	2. False	3. True
4. True	5. False	6. False
7. True	8. False	9. False
10. True	11. False	12. False
13. True	14. True	15. False
16. True	17. True	18. True
19. True	20. True	

APPROPRIATE TERM

1. Three way cross
2. Triallel analysis
3. Double cross
4. Quadriallel analysis

●●●

10

CHAPTER

Generation Mean Analysis

A. DEFINITIONS

Generation mean analysis. The biometrical analysis which is based on the mean values of six populations *viz.* P_1, P_2, F_1, F_2, B_1 and B_2 generation of a cross between two pure lines having contrasting characters. There are three models of generation mean analysis, *viz.* six parameter model, five parameter model and three parameter model.

Six Parameter model. A model or procedure of generation mean analysis which provides information about six parameters, *viz.* m, d, h, i, j and l.

Five Parameter model. A model of generation mean analysis which provides information about five parameters, *viz.* m, d, h, i and l. This model involves P_1, P_2, F_1, F_2 and F_3 populations of a cross in analysis.

Three parameter model. A model of generation mean analysis which provides information about three parameters, *viz.* m, d and h.

Scaling test. In generation mean analysis, a test which is used to find out the presence or absence of epistasis.

Joint scaling test. In generation mean analysis, a test which permits any combination of the six population. It provides information about presence or absence of epistasis as well as about m, d and h parameters.

Degree of dominance. It refers to the ratio of dominance variance to additive variance *viz.* $\sqrt{H/D}$. If this ratio is zero, there is no dominance, if it is greater than zero but lesser than one, there is partial dominance, if it is equal to one, there is complete dominance, and if it is greater than one, it indicates over dominance.

B. BACKGROUND INFORMATION

1. The concept of generation mean analysis was developed by Hayman (1958) and Jinks and Jones (1958).

2. The six parameter model was proposed by Hayman (1958).
3. Analysis of six parameter model is based on six populations (P_1, P_2, F_1, F_2, B_1 and B_2) of the single cross.
4. Six parameter model provides information about six parameters *viz.* mean (*m*) additive effects (*d*), dominance effects (*h*), and additive × additive (*i*), additive × dominance (*j*) and dominance × dominance (*l*) types of epistasis.
5. Testing of six parameter model with X^2 test is not possible.
6. Five parameter model was also provided by Hayman (1958).
7. Analysis of five parameter model is based on five populations *viz.* P_1, P_2, F_1, F_2 and F_3 of a cross.
8. Five parameter model does not provide information about additive × dominance type of epistasis.
9. Five parameter model is used when back cross populations (B_1 and B_2) are not available and instead F_3 population of a cross is available.
10. Five parameter model provides X^2 test for testing of model.
11. Three parameter model was proposed by Jinks and Jones. (1958).
12. Three parameter model is used when epistasis is absent.
13. Analysis of three parameter model is based on six populations (P_1, P_2, F_1, F_2, B_1 and B_2) of a cross.
14. In three parameter model, testing of model with X^2 test is not possible.
15. In the absence of epistasis, Mather (1949) provided method of estimating additive, dominance and environmental variances from general means of a cross.
16. Mather (1949) provided four types of scaling tests, *viz.* A, B, C and D.
17. The significance of any of the four scaling tests indicates the presence of epistasis.
18. The significance of (A) and (B) scales indicates presence of all three types of epistasis *i.e.* additive × additive, additive × dominance and dominance × dominance.
19. The significance of C scale suggests dominance × dominance type of epistasis.
20. The significance of D scale reveals additive × additive type of epistasis.
21. The significance of C and D scales indicates additive × additive and dominance × dominance types of epistasis.
22. Joint scaling test was proposed by Cavalli (1952).
23. Similar sign of *h* and *l* components indicates presence of complementary epistasis.
24. Opposite sign of *h* and *l* components indicates duplicate epistasis.
25. Generation mean analysis is free from genetical assumptions.
26. In generation mean analysis, combining ability analysis is not possible.
27. Generation mean analysis evaluates two inbreds at a time.
28. There are three models of generation mean analysis, *viz.*, six, five and three parameter models.
29. Generation mean analysis is based on first order statistics.
30. Generation mean analysis evaluated one cross at a time.

C. MULTIPLE CHOICE

1. The concept of generation mean analysis was developed in 1958 by :

(a) Hayman (b) Jinks and Jones
(c) (a) and (b) (d) Griffing.

2. Hayman and Jinks and Jones developed the concept of generation mean analysis in :

(a) 1936 (b) 1954
(c) 1958 (d) 1962.

3. The six parameter model was proposed in 1958 by :

(a) Griffing (b) Hayman
(c) Kempthorne (d) None of these.

4. Hayman proposed the six parameter model in :

(a) 1921 (b) 1936
(c) 1954 (d) 1958.

5. Analysis of six parameter model is based on

(a) Three populations (b) Four populations
(c) Five populations (d) Six populations.

6. Six parameter model provides information about which of the following parameters :

(a) m and d (b) h and i
(c) j and l (d) All of these.

7. Five parameter model was proposed in 1958 by :

(a) Mather (b) Falconer
(c) Hayman (d) Jinks.

8. F_3 population is used in analysis instead of B_1 and B_2 in :

(a) Six parameter model (b) Five parameter model
(c) Three parameter model (d) All of these.

9. Which type of epistasis is not estimated in five parameter model ?

(a) Additive × additive (b) Additive × dominance
(c) Dominance × dominance (d) All of these.

10. Five parameter model provides information about which of the following estimates :

(a) m and d (b) d and h
(c) i and l (d) All of these.

11. Three parameter model was proposed in 1958 by :

(a) Mather (b) Mather and Jinks
(c) Jinks and Jones (d) All of these.

12. Three parameter model was proposed by Jinks and Jones in :

(a) 1936 (b) 1943
(c) 1958 (d) 1962.

13. Analysis of three parameter model is based on which of the following populations :

(a) P_1, P_2, F_1, F_2 (b) B_1, B_2, F_3
(c) P_1, P_2, B_1, B_2 (d) P_1, P_2, F_1, F_2, B_1 and B_2.

14. Who provided method of estimating additive, dominance and environmental variances in 1949, in the absence of epistasis ?

(a) Mather (b) Mather and Jinks
(c) Hayman (d) Jinks and Jones.

15. Scaling test was proposed in 1949 by :

(a) Smith (b) Hayman
(c) Mather (d) Griffing.

16. Scaling tests are of :

(a) Two types (b) Three types
(c) Four types (d) Five types.

17. Which type of epistasis is indicated when (A) and (B) scales are significant.

(a) Additive × additive (b) Additive × dominance
(c) Dominance × dominance (d) All of these.

18. What type of epistasis is expected when C scale is significant

(a) Additive × additive (b) Additive × dominance
(c) Dominance × dominance (d) All of these.

19. What type of epistasis is expected when D scale is significant ?

(a) Additive × additive (b) Additive × dominance
(c) Dominance × dominance (d) None of these.

20. What type of epistasis is expected when both C and D Scales are significant ?

(a) Dominance × dominance (b) Additive × additive
(c) (a) and (b) (d) Additive × dominance.

21. Joint scaling test was proposed in 1952 by :

(a) Mather (b) Jinks
(c) Cavalli (d) Hayman.

22. Cavalli proposed the joint scaling test in :

(a) 1921 (b) 1936
(c) 1952 (d) 1958.

23. What type of epistasis is expected when signs of h and l are similar ?

(a) Duplicate (b) Complementary
(c) Supplementary (d) All of these.

24. What type of epistasis is expected when signs of h and l are opposite ?

(a) Complementary (b) Inhibiting
(c) Duplicate (d) Supplementary.

25. Which of the following estimates is not possible through generation mean analysis :

(a) Additive variance (b) Dominance variance
(c) Epistatic variance (d) Combining ability.

26. If the ratio of dominance variance to additive variance is zero, there will be :

(a) No dominance (b) Partial dominance
(c) Complete dominance (d) Over dominance.

D. FILL IN THE BLANKS

1. Concept of generation mean was developed by ....
2. The six parameter model of generation mean analysis was proposed by ....
3. Six parameter model was proposed in ....
4. Analysis of six parameter is based on .... populations.
5. Five parameter model was provided by ....
6. Five parameter model was proposed by Hayman in ....
7. Analysis of five parameter model is based on .... populations.
8. In place of B_1 and B_2 generations F_3 is used in .... model.
9. Three parameter model was proposed by ....
10. Three parameter model was proposed in ....
11. When epistasis is absent, ... parameter model is used.
12. Analysis of three parameter model is based on .... populations.
13. The scaling test was provided by ....
14. Mather provided scaling test in ....
15. The significance of C scale suggests .... epistasis.
16. The significance of D scale suggests .... epistasis.
17. The joint scaling test was proposed by ....
18. Cavalli proposed joint scaling test in ....
19. Similar sign of *h* and *l* indicates presence of .... epistasis.
20. Opposite sign of *h* and *l* indicates presence of .... epistasis.
21. Generation mean analysis is based on .... statistics.
22. Generation mean analysis evaluates .... inbeds at a time.

E. MARK TRUE OR FALSE

1. Concept of generation mean analysis was developed by Fisher.
2. The six parameter model was proposed by Hayman.
3. The Analysis of six parameter model is based on P_1, P_2, F_1, F_2 and F_3 populations.
4. Five parameter model was proposed by Jinks.
5. Five parameter model involves P_1, P_2, F_1, F_2, B_1 and B_2 In the analysis.
6. Six parameter model provides X^2 test for testing of model.
7. Five parameter model does not provide X^2 for testing of model.
8. Three parameter model was proposed by Jinks and Jones.
9. Analysis of three parameter model is based on six populations.
10. The scaling test was provided by Hayman.
11. Hayman proposed scaling test in 1949.
12. Significance of C scale indicates dominance × dominance type of epistasis.

13. Significance of D scale indicates A × A and A × D type of epistasis.
14. The significance of C and D scales reveals A × A type of epistasis.
15. Joint scaling test was provided by Cavalli.
16. Cavalli proposed joint scaling test in 1940.
17. Opposite sign of *h* and *l* components indicates complementary epistasis.
18. Similar sign of *h* and *l* indicates duplicate epistasis.
19. Generation mean analysis is based on second order statistics.
20. Generation mean analysis permits evaluation of one cross at a time.
21. Generation mean analysis is free from genetical assumptions.
22. Significance of scaling test indicates absence of epistasis.

F. USE APPROPRIATE TERM

1. Biometrical analysis involving six populations of a cross between two pure lines. (P_1, P_2, F_1, F_2, B_1 and B_2).
2. A model of generation mean analysis which provides information about six parameters. (*m, d, h, i, j* and *l*).
3. A model of generation mean analysis which provides information about five parameters. (*m, d, h, i,* and *l*).
4. A model of generation mean analysis which provides information about three parameters (*m, d* and *h*).
5. In generation mean analysis, a test which is used to detect the presence or absence of epistatis.
6. The ratio of dominance variance to additive variance.

ANSWERS

MULTIPLE CHOICE

1. (c) (a) and (b)
2. (c) 1958
3. (b) Hayman
4. (d) 1958
5. (d) Six populations
6. (d) All of these
7. (c) Hayman
8. (b) Five parameter model
9. (b) Additive × additive
10. (d) All of these
11. (c) Jinks and Jones
12. (c) 1958
13. (d) P_1, P_2, F_1, F_2, B_1 and B_2
14. (a) Mather
15. (c) Mather
16. (c) Four types
17. (d) All of these
18. (c) Dominance × dominance
19. (a) Additive × additive
20. (c) (a) and (b)
21. (c) Cavalli
22. (c) 1952
23. (b) Complementary
24. (c) Duplicate
25. (d) Combining ability
26. (a) No dominance

FILL IN THE BLANKS

1. Hayman, Jinks and Jones
2. Hayman

3. 1958
4. Six
5. Hayman
6. 1958
7. Five
8. Five parameter
9. Jinks and Jones
10. 1958
11. Three
12. Six
13. Mather
14. 1949
15. Dominance × dominance
16. Additive × additive
17. Cavalli
18. 1952
19. Complementary
20. Duplicate
21. First order
22. Two

TRUE OR FALSE

1. False
2. True
3. False
4. False
5. False
6. False
7. False
8. True
9. True
10. False
11. False
12. True
13. False
14. False
15. True
16. False
17. False
18. False
19. False
20. True
21. True
22. False

APPROPRIATE TERM

1. Generation mean analysis
2. Six parameter model
3. Five Parameter model
4. Three parameter model
5. Scaling test
6. Degree of dominance.

●●●

11 CHAPTER

Biparental Mating and Triple Test Cross

A. DEFINITIONS

Biparental cross. Crossing of randomly selected plants in F_2 or subsequent generation of a cross between two pure lines in a definite portion. There are three mating designs of biparental cross *viz.* North Carolina Design 1 (NCD-1), North Carolina Design 2 (NCD_2), and North Carolina Design 3 (NCD 3).

NCD 1. A design of biparental cross in which in F_2 each male is mated to a different group of females resulting in *f* crosses, where *f* is the number of female plants used for crossing in a set.

NCD 2. A design of biparental cross in which in F_2 each selected male is mated (crossed) to the same group of female plants resulting in *mf* crosses, where *m* and *f* denote number of male and female plants per set.

NCD 3. A design of biparental cross in which in F_2 each randomly selected male plant is mated with P_1 and P_2 parents of original cross resulting in 2 *m* crosses, where *m* is the number of male plants used per set.

Mating. The process of crossing between selected parents or plants.

Set. Number of single crosses obtained by crossing randomly selected one group of male and female parents in a definite portion.

Test cross. In strict sense, crossing of F_1 with its homozygous recessive parent. In quantitative genetics, various crosses made using a common tester are called test crosses. Crossing F_1 with its homozygous recessive parent is called simple or single test cross. Crossing of F_1 with both parents (P_1 and P_2) is called double test cross.

Triple test cross. Crossing of randomly selected F_2 plants with both the parents (P_1 and P_2) involved in the cross, and with their F_1 hybrid.

B. BACKGROUND INFORMATION

1. The concept of biparental cross was originally developed by Constock and Robinson (1948, 1952).
2. The analysis of biparental cross involves F_2, P_1 and P_2 populations of a single cross.
3. Biparental cross analysis provides information about additive variance and dominance variance.
4. Biparental cross analysis does not provide estimates of epistatic variance.
5. Biparental mating is very effective in breaking undesirable linkages, creating genetic variability and improving adaptation of a population.
6. Biparental mating does not permit simultaneous evaluation of several segregating crosses.
7. The analysis of biparental cross is based on eight genetic assumptions, *viz.* (*i*) random distribution of genetypes in relation to variation, (*ii*) random choice of plants in F_2 for mating, (*iii*) diploid segregation, (*iv*) absence of maternal effects, (*v*) lack of multiple alleles, (*vi*) absence of linkage, (*vii*) absence of epistasis, and (*viii*) equal survival of all genotypes. However, all these assumptions are seldom fulfilled.
8. NCD 1 is also known as nested design.
9. Designs of biparental mating are also know as North Carolina Designs.
10. In NCD 1, each male plant is mated to a different set of female plants.
11. In NCD 1 each set consists of f crosses, where f is the number of female plants.
12. In NCD 1, the variance is divided into two fractions, *viz.* variance among males (¼VA), and variance due to females (¼VA + ¼VD).
13. NCD 1, is influenced by the presence of maternal effects.
14. NCD 1, is the least powerful design.
15. NCD 2 is similar to line × tester cross and is also known as factorial design.
16. In NCD 2, each selected male is mated to the same set of female plants.
17. In NCD 2, each set consists of mf crosses where m and f denote number of male and female plants.
18. In NCD 2, the variance among single crosses is divided into three fractions, *viz.* variance due to males (¼VA), and variance due to females (¼VA), and variance due to males × females (¼VA).
19. NCD 2 is also influenced by the presence of maternal effects.
20. NCD 2 is an intermediate design.
21. In NCD 3, each selected male is mated to both parents of original cross.
22. In NCD 3, each set consists of 2 m crosses, where *m* is the member of male plants used in a set.
23. In NCD 3, variance among single crosses is divided into two fractions, *viz.* variance among males (½VA) and variance due to males × females (½VD).
24. NCD 3 is not affected by the presence of maternal effects.
25. NCD 3 is the most powerful design.

26. NCD 3 requires much lesser area than designs 1 and 2.
27. NCD 3 involves F_2, P_1 and P_2 plants in crossing.
28. NCD 1 and NCD 2 involve F_2 plants in crossing.
29. The concept of triple test cross (TTC) analysis was poroposed by Kearsey and Jinks (1968).
30. Triple test cross analysis involves P_1, P_2, F_1 and F_2 populations of a single cross.
31. TTC provides information about the presence or absence of epistasis.
32. TTC is an extension of North Carolina Design 3.
33. In TTC, selected F_2 plants are backcrossed to both the inbred parents (P_1 and P_2) and their F_1.
34. TTC involves 4 populations (P_1, P_2, F_1 and F_2).

C. MULTIPLE CHOICE

1. The concept of biparental mating was developed in 1948 by :
   (a) Mather and Jinks (b) Comstock and Robinson
   (c) Jinks and Jones (d) Jinks and Hayman.
2. In which year the concept of biparental cross was developed ?
   (a) 1934 (b) 1948
   (c) 1962 (d) 1968.
3. Which of the following designs is called nested design ?
   (a) NCD 1 (b) NCD 2
   (c) NCD 3 (d) None of these.
4. Which of the following designs of biparental cross is known as factorial design ?
   (a) NCD 1 (b) NCD 2
   (c) NCD 3 (d) None of these.
5. Which of the following designs is the most powerful one ?
   (a) NCD 1 (b) NCD 2
   (c) NCD 3 (d) All of these.
6. Biparental cross does not provide information about :
   (a) Additive variance (b) Dominance variance
   (c) Epistatic variance (d) All of these.
7. Which of the following designs is similar to line × tester cross ?
   (a) NCD 1 (b) NCD 2
   (c) NCD 3 (d) None of these.
8. Which of the following designs is the least powerful ?
   (a) NCD 1 (b) NCD 2
   (c) NCD 3 (d) None of these.
9. Which of the following designs is not influenced by maternal effects ?
   (a) NCD 1 (b) NCD 2
   (c) NCD 3 (d) All of these.

10. Which of the following design involves F_1, P_1 and P_2 populations ?
(a) NCD 1 (b) NCD 2
(c) NCD 3 (d) None of these.

11. How many genetical assumptions are there for biparental cross ?
(a) Three (b) Five
(c) Six (d) Eight.

12. The NCD 3 involves :
(a) F_2 (b) F_2, P_1 and P_2
(c) Bc_1 and Bc_2 (d) None of these.

13. Variance due to males is = ¼VA in :
(a) NCD 1 (b) NCD 2
(c) (a) and (b) (d) None of these.

14. Variance due to males is = ½VA in :
(a) NCD 1 (b) NCD 2
(c) NCD 3 (d) All of these.

15. Variance due to males × female is = ½VD in :
(a) NCD 1 (b) NCD 2
(c) NCD 3 (d) None of these.

16. Variance due to females is = ¼VA in :
(a) NCD 1 (b) NCD 2
(c) NCD 3 (d) None of these.

17. Variance due to females is = ¼VA + ¼VD in :
(a) NCD 1 (b) NCD 2
(c) NCD 3 (d) All of these.

18. Each set of NCD 3 consists of how many crosses ?
(a) 2 m (b) mf
(c) f (d) All of these.

19. How many crosses are there in each set of NCD 2 :
(a) f (b) 2 m
(c) mf (d) None of these.

20. All genetical assumptions of biparental analysis are fulfilled
(a) Always (b) Never
(c) Seldom (d) All of these.

21. The concept of triple test cross analysis was proposed in 1968 by :
(a) Mather and Jinks (b) Jinks and Jones
(c) Kearsey and Jinks (d) Hayman.

22. Kearsey and Jinks proposed the concept of TTC analysis in :
(a) 1947 (b) 1954
(c) 1968 (d) 1975.

23. TTC provides information about :
(a) Additive variance (b) Dominance variance
(c) Presence/absence of epistasis (d) All of these.

24. TTC is an extension of :
(a) NCD 1 (b) NCD 2
(c) NCD 3 (d) None of these.

25. In TTC selected F_2 plants are backcrossed to :
(a) P_1 (b) P_2
(c) P_1 and P_2 (d) P_1, P_2 and F_1.

26. How many populations are involved in TTC analysis :
(a) One (b) Two
(c) Three (d) Four.

27. Which of the following populations are required for TTC analysis ?
(a) P_1 (b) P_1 and P_2
(c) P_1, P_2 and F_1 (d) P_1, P_2, F_1 and F_2.

D. FILL IN THE BLANKS

1. Concept of biparental mating was developed by ....

2. North Carolina Designs (NCD) refer ....

3. Robinson and Comstock developed the concept of be biparental mating in ....

4. NCD 1 is also known as ....

5. NCD 2 is also called ....

6. Analysis of biparental cross involves .... population of a cross.

7. Biparental mating does not provide estimates of ....

8. In NCD 1, variance among males is equal to ....

9. NCD 1 is influenced by the presence of ....

10. NCD 1 is the least .... design.

11. NCD 2 is similar to ....cross.

12. NCD 3 is not affected by the passence of ....

13. NCD 3 is the most .... design.

14. NCD 3 involves .... populations in crossing.

15. NCD 1 and NCD 2 involve .... populations in crossing.

16. In NCD 2, variance due to males is equal to ....

17. In NCD 3, variance among males is equal to ....

18. The concept of triple test cross (TTC) was developed by ....

19. Concept of TTC was developed in ....

20. TTC involves .... populations of a single cross.

21. TTC provide information about the presence or absence of ....

22. TTC an extension of ....

E. MARK TRUE OR FALSE

1. Mather developed the concept of biparental mating in 1949.
2. Biparental analysis involves F_2, P_1 and P_2 populations of a cross.
3. Biparental cross is also called South Carolina Design.
4. NCD 1 is also called factorial design.
5. NCD 2 is also known as nested design.
6. NCD 1 is influenced by the presence of maternal effects.
7. NCD 1 is the least powerful design.
8. NCD 2 is the most powerful design.
9. NCD 2 is similar to line × tester cross.
10. In NCD 1, each male plant is mated to the same set of female plants.
11. In NCD 2, each male plant is mated to the different set of female plants.
12. NCD 3 is not affected by the presence of maternal effects.
13. NCD 3 is an intermediate design.
14. NCD 3 requires more area than NCD 1 and NCD 2.
15. NCD 3 involves F_2, P_1 and P_2 plants of a cross in mating.
16. The concept of TTC was developed by Kempthorne.
17. The concept of TTC was developed in 1968.
18. TTC provides information about presence or absence of epistasis.
19. In TTC 3, variance due to males × females is equal to $\frac{1}{4}$VD.
20. TTC is an extension of North Carolina Design 3.
21. In NCD 1, each set consists of f crosses where f is the number of female plants.
22. In NCD 2, each set consists of mf crosses where m and f are male and female plants.

F. USE APPROPRIATE TERM

1. Crossing of randomly selected plants in F_2 or subsequent generation of a cross between two puro lines in a definite fashion.
2. The process of crossing between selected plants or parents.
3. In quantitative genetics, various crosses made using a common tester.
4. Crossing of randomly selected F_2 plants with both the parents (P_1 and P_2) involved in tho cross and with their F_1 hybrid.

ANSWERS

MULTIPLE CHOICE

1. (b) Comstock and Robinson
2. (b) 1948
3. (a) NCD 1
4. (b) NCD 2
5. (c) NCD 3
6. (c) Epistatic variance
7. (b) NCD 2
8. (a) NCD 1
9. (c) NCD 3

10. (c) NCD 3
11. (d) Eight
12. (b) F_2, P_1 and P_2
13. (c) (a) and (b)
14. (c) NCD 3
15. (c) NCD 3
16. (b) NCD 2
17. (a) NCD 1
18. (a) 2m
19. (c) mf
20. (c) Seldom
21. (c) Kearsey and Jinks
22. (c) 1968
23. (d) All of these
24. (c) NCD 3
25. (d) P_1, P_2 and F_1
26. (c) Three
27. (d) P_1, P_2, F_1, F_2

FILL IN THE BLANKS

1. Comstock and Robinson
2. Biparental mating
3. 1948, 1952
4. Nested design
5. Factorial design
6. F_2, P_1 and P_2
7. Epistatic variance
8. $\frac{1}{4}$VA
9. Maternal effects
10. Powerful
11. Line × tester
12. Maternal effects
13. Powerful
14. F_2, P_1 and P_2
15. F_2
16. $\frac{1}{4}$VA
17. $\frac{1}{2}$VA
18. Kearsey and Jinks
19. 1968
20. P_1, P_2, F_1 and F_2
21. Epistasis
22. NCD 3

TRUE OR FALSE

1. False	2. True	3. False
4. False	5. False	6. True
7. True	8. False	9. True
10. False	11. False	12. True
13. False	14. False	15. True
16. False	17. True	18. True
19. False	20. True	21. True
22. True		

APPROPRIATE TERM

1. Biparental cross
2. Mating
3. Test crosses
4. Triple test cross.

●●●

12
CHAPTER

Analysis of Adaptation and Stability

A. DEFINITIONS

Environment. External conditions which affect expression of genes of an individual or genotype. It includes topography, soil type, day length, temperature, rainfall, relative humidity, etc. The environment is of two types *viz.* micro environment and macro environment.

Micro-environment. Environment of a single genotype as opposed to another genotype growing at the same time in the same place.

Micro-environment. Environmental differences which are easily detectable such as effect of fertilizer doses, planting dates, spacings, irrigation, etc.

Predictable factors. Factors which are under human control, *viz.* planting date, row spacing, plant population, fertilizer doses etc.

Unpredictable factors. Factors which fluctuate inconsistently and are not under human control such a rainfall, temperature, relative humidity, etc.

Adaptation. The fitness of a genotype or population to a given environment or the process of adjustment of organisms to the changes occurring in the environment. Adaptation is of following four types.

Specific genotypic adaptation. Adaptation of a genotype to a limited environment such as floating rice.

General genotypic adaptation. Capacity of a genotype to produce a wide range of phenotypes compatible with a range of environment. Examples are semidwarf varieties of wheat and rice.

Specific population adaptation. The capacity of a heterogeneous population to adapt to the specific environment. Examples are composite variety and varietal blends.

General population adaptation. The capacity of a heterogeneous population to adapt to a wide range of environments. Example is synthetic varieties.

Adaptability. The capacity of a genotype or population for genetic change in adaptation.

Stability. Suitability of a variety for general cultivation over a wide range of environmental conditions or stable performance of a variety in various environments.

Homeostasis. The buffering capacity of a genotype to environmental fluctuation. Adaptability is a result of homeostasis. Homeostasis is of two types, *viz.* genetic and physiological.

Genetic homeostasis. The genetic buffering capacity of a genotype to environmental fluctuations.

Physiological homeostasis. The physiological or developmental buffering capacity of a genotype to environmental fluctuations. It includes internal self regulatory mechanisms.

Genetic polymorphism. Regular occurrence of several phenotypes in a genetic population due to superiority of heterozygotes over homozygotes, also called balanced polymorphism.

Balanced polymorphism. Polymorphism which results due to heterozygote advantage or due to better survival of heterozygotes over homozygotes.

Stability parameters. Stability parameters include mean yield over environments, regression coefficient and deviation from regression.

Coadaptation. The selection process for a balanced combination of genes in an individual or selection process for harmoniously interacting individuals in a population.

Adaptedness. The degree of suitability of an organisms to its environment, developed overtime as a result of selection.

B. BACKGROUND INFORMATION

1. The terms macro and micro environments were given by Comstock and Moll in 1963.
2. The varietal adaptability is measured in terms of phenotypic stability *i.e.* genotype × environmental interaction.
3. Physiological homeostasis is generally higher in heterozygous genotypes than in homozygous genotypes.
4. The adaptability of a genotype is influenced by four main factors, *viz.* heterogeneity, heterozygosity, genetic polymorphism and genetic base.
5. The low magnitude of G × E interaction indicates consistent performance of a population over variable environments.
6. The first systematic approach for stability analysis of cultivars was made by Finlay and Wilkinson in 1963.
7. Finlay and Wilkinson (1963) used two parameters for stability *viz.* mean yield over locations and regression coefficient.
8. Based on value of regression coefficient, Finlay and Wilkinson gave four types of stability, *viz.* average stability (b = 1), below average stability (b > 1), above average stability (b < 1) and absolute stability (b = 0).

9. In Finlay and Wilkinson (1963) model, deviations from the regression line are not estimated.
10. According to Eberhart and Russell (1966), a stable variety has regression coefficient of unity (b = 1) and minimum deviation from regression line ($sd^2 = 0$).
11. In 1971, Freeman and Perkins proposed a model of stability analysis which permits independent estimation of mean performance and environmental index.
12. The stability analysis model proposed by Eberhart and Russell (1966) is most widely used because it is relatively simple yet quite informative.
13. The term homeostasis was coined by Lerner in 1954.
14. Genetic polymorphisms is also called balanced polymorphism.
15. Adaptability is the result of homeostasis.
16. Genotypes with broad genetic base wider adaptability.
17. General genotypic and general population adaptations are examples of wide adaptability.
18. Adaptable genotypes produce narrow range of phenotypes in different environments.
19. Natural selection plays important role in the process of adaptation.
20. Human selection plays important role in combining adaptability and productivity.
21. A more homeostatic genotype exhibits less variation in phenotypic values in different environments.
22. Genetic polymorphism increases the adaptive value or buffering capacity of a population by producing increased diversity of genotypes in a population.
23. Heterozygosity in a population promotes homeostasis.
24. Stability analysis is carried out with multilocational or multiseasonal data or both.
25. The estimates of stability are based on first order statistics.
26. Stability analysis is usually performed with varietes and hybrids.
27. Diverse (heterogeneous) populations give more stable yields over several environments than pureline.
28. Stability analysis is useful in predicting varietal response under different environments.
29. The term coadaptation was coined by Dobzhansky in 1950.

C. MULTIPLE CHOICES

1. Terms micro and macro environments were given in 1963 by :
   (a) Mather and Jinks (b) Comstock and Moll
   (c) Comstock and Robinson (d) Fisher and Yates.
2. Environment of a single genotype is called :
   (a) Mega-environment (b) Macro-environment
   (c) Micro-environment (d) None of these.
3. Predictable factors include :
   (a) Planting date (b) Spacings
   (c) Fertilizer doses (d) All of these.

4. Unpredictable factors include :
(a) Rainfall (b) Temperature
(c) Relative humidity (d) All of these.

5. Which of the following factors is unpredictable ?
(a) Row spacing (b) Irrigation
(c) Rainfall (d) Fertilizer dose.

6. Which of the following factors is predictable ?
(a) Temperature (b) Relative humidity
(c) Rainfall (d) Sowing date.

7. Which of the following factors is under human control ?
(a) Irrigation (b) Sowing date
(c) Fertilizer dose (d) All of these.

8. Which of the following factors is not under human control ?
(a) Rainfall (b) Temperature
(c) Relative humidity (d) All of these.

9. Fitness of a genotype to a given environment is called :
(a) Stability (b) Adaptability
(c) Adaptation (d) Co-adaptation.

10. The capacity of genotype for genetic change in adaptation is called :
(a) Stability (b) Adaptability
(c) Co-adaptation (d) Adaptation.

11. The suitability of a genotype for general cultivation over a wide range of environment is known as :
(a) Heritability (b) Stability
(c) Adaptability (d) None of these.

12. Floating rice is an example of :
(a) Specific genotypic adaptation (b) General genotypic adaptation
(c) Specific population adaptation (d) General population adaptation.

13. Composite variety is an example of :
(a) Specific genotypic adaptation (b) General genotypic adaptation
(c) Specific population adaptation (d) General population adaptation.

14. Which of the following has specific population adaptation ?
(a) Synthetic variety (b) Composite variety
(c) Floating rice (d) Semidwarf wheat.

15. Which of the following is an example of specific genotypic adaptation ?
(a) Synthetic variety (b) Floating rice
(c) Semidwarf rice (d) Composite variety.

16. Which of the following has general genotypic adaptation ?
(a) Composite variety (b) Synthetic variety
(c) Semidwarf wheat (d) All of these.

17. The example of general population adaptation is :
(a) Floating rice (b) Semidwarf wheat
(c) Synthetic variety (d) Varietal blends.

18. Examples of specific population adaptation refer to :
(a) Composite variety
(b) Varietal blends
(c) (a) and (b)
(d) Synthetic variety.

19. The term homeostasis was coined in 1954 by :
(a) Mather
(b) Falconer
(c) Lerner
(d) Comstock.

20. The first systematic approach for stability analysis of cultivars was made by :
(a) Finlay and Wilkinson
(b) Eberhart and Russell
(c) Perkins and Jinks
(d) Freeman and Perkins

21. Finlay and Wilkinson proposed model of stability analysis in :
(a) 1963
(b) 1966
(c) 1968
(d) 1971.

22. Eberhart and Russell proposed their model of stability analysis in :
(a) 1953
(b) 1963
(c) 1966
(d) 1971.

23. Freeman and Perkins proposed their model of stability analysis in :
(a) 1963
(b) 1966
(c) 1968
(d) 1971.

24. Perkins and Jinks proposed their model of stability analysis in :
(a) 1954
(b) 1966
(c) 1968
(d) 1971.

25. Which of the following stability analysis models does not permit estimation of deviations from the regression line ?
(a) Finlay and Wilkinson model
(b) Eberhart and Russell model
(c) Perkins and Jinks model
(d) Freeman and Perkins model.

26. The adaptability of a genotype is influenced by :
(a) Genetic diversity
(b) Heterozygosity
(c) Genetic polymorphism
(d) All of these.

27. The buffering capacity of a population showing low magnitude of G × E interaction would be :
(a) High
(b) Low
(c) Medium
(d) Zero.

28. Independent estimation of mean performance and environmental index is possible in the stability analysis model given by :
(a) Finlay and Wilkinson
(b) Eberhart and Russell
(c) Perkins and Jinks
(d) Freeman and Perkins.

29. In Finlay and Wilkinson model, the regression coefficient of unity ($b = 1$) indicates :
(a) Average stability
(b) Above average stability
(c) Below average stability
(d) Absolute stability.

30. In Finlay and Wilkinson model, what will be the value of regression coefficient for average stability ?
(a) $b = \perp$
(b) $b = > \perp$
(c) $b = < \perp$
(d) $b = 0$.

31. The zero value of regression coefficient (b = 0) in Finlay and Wilkinson model indicates :

(a) Below average stability
(b) Average stability
(c) Above average stability
(d) Absolute stability.

32. Which of the following stability analysis is most commonly used in plant breeding ?

(a) Finlay and Wilkinson model
(b) Eberhart and Russell model
(c) Perkins and Jinks model
(d) Freeman and Perkins model.

33. The selection process for balanced combination of genes in an individual is called :

(a) Adaptation
(b) Coadaptation
(c) Adaptability
(d) Stability.

34. The term coadaptation was coined in 1950 by :

(a) Stebbins
(b) Dobzhansky
(c) Darwin
(d) Mendel.

35. The degree of suitability of an organism to its environment is called :

(a) Adaptation
(b) Coadaptation
(c) Adaptedness
(d) Adaptability.

36. Stability parameters include :

(a) Mean yield
(b) Regression coefficient
(c) Deviation from regression
(d) All of these.

37. Adaptability is the result of :

(a) Homeostasis
(b) Homeosis
(c) Heteropycnosis
(d) None of these.

38. Homeostasis is associated with :

(a) Heterozygosity
(b) Genetic diversity
(c) Genetic polymorphism
(d) All of these.

39. Stability analysis is based on :

(a) One season data
(b) Multi seasonal data
(c) Multi locational data
(d) (b) and (c).

40. Genotypes with broad genetic base have :

(a) Poor adaptability
(b) Average stability
(c) Wide adaptability
(d) None of these.

D. FILL IN THE BLANKS

1. Terms micro and macro environment were coined by ....
2. Comstock and Moll first used terms micro and macro environments in ....
3. The stability analysis was first suggested by ....
4. Deviations from regression are not estimated in .... model.
5. Eberhart and Russell proposed a model of stability analysis in ....
6. Eberhart and Russell first used stability analysis in .... crop.
7. Freeman and Perkins proposed a model of stability analysis in ....

8. .... model permits independent estimation of mean performance and environment index.
9. The .... model of stability analysis in widely used.
10. Perkins and Jinks proposed a model of stability analysis in ....
11. The term genetic homeostasis was coined by ....
12. Lerner coined the term genetic homeostasis in ....
13. Adaptability is the result of ....
14. Genetic polymorphism is also called ....
15. Genotypes with broad genetic base have ....
16. Heterozygosity in a population promotes ....
17. Estimates of stability are based on .... statistics.
18. Stability analysis is performed with .... data.
19. Diverse populations are .... than purelines.
20. The term coadaptation was coined by ....
21. Dobzhansky coined the term coadaptation in ....
22. Floating rice is an example of ....
23. Composite variety is an example of ....
24. Synthetic variety is an example of ....
25. Semidwarf varieties of wheat and rice are examples of ....
26. Easily detectable environmental differences refer to ....
27. Minute environmental differences refer to ....
28. Factors which are under human control refer to ....

E. MARK TRUE OR FALSE

1. Terms micro and macro environments were coined by Dobzhansky.
2. Stability analysis was first suggested by Eberhart and Russell.
3. Finlay and Wilkinson model does not permit estimation of deviations from regression.
4. Eberhart and Russell first used stability analysis in barley.
5. The Perkins and Jinks model is most widely used.
6. Freeman and Perkins model permits independent estimation of mean performance and environmental index.
7. Adaptability is more in heterogeneous populations than homogeneous populations.
8. Heterozygous populations are less adaptable than homozygous populations.
9. The term genetic homeostasis was coined by Muller.
10. The term coadaptation was coined by Dobzhansky.

11. Homeostasis promotes adaptability.
12. Genotypes with broad genetic base have narrow adaptation.
13. Adaptable genotypes produce narrow range of phenotypes in different environment.
14. Natural selection improves adaptation.
15. An adaptable genotype exhibits less variation in phenotypic values in different environments.
16. Genetic polymorphism leads to increase in adaptation.
17. Adaptability analysis is based on high order statistics.
18. Diverse populations are more adaptable than purelines or inbed lines.
19. Floating rice is an example of specific genotypic adaptation.
20. Composite variety is an example of general population adaptation.
21. Synthetic variety is an example of specific population adaptation.
22. Semidwarf varieties of wheat and rice are examples of general genotypic adaptation.

F. USE APPROPRIATE TERM

1. External conditions which affect expression of genes in a genotype.
2. Environment of a single genotype.
3. Environment differences which are easily detectable.
4. Factors which are under human control.
5. Factors which are controlled by nature.
6. Fitness of a genotype or population to a given environment or the process of adjustment of organisms to the changes occurring in the environment.
7. Adaptation of a genotype to a particular environment.
8. Adaptation of a genotype to the wide range of environments.
9. Adaptation of a population to the specific environment.
10. Adaptation of a population to the wide range of environments.
11. The capacity of a genotype or population for genetic change in adaptation.
12. Suitability of a variety for general cultivation over a wide range of environmental conditions.
13. The buffering capacity of a genotype to environmental fluctuations.
14. Genetic buffering capacity of a genotype to environmental changes.
15. Physiological or developmental buffering capacity of a genotype to environmental fluctuations.
16. Regular occurrence of several phenotypes in a genetic population due to superiority of heterozygotes over homozygotes.
17. Polymorphism due to heterozygote advantage.
18. The selection process for a balanced combination of genes in an individual.

ANSWERS

MULTIPLE CHOICE

1. (b) Comstock and Moll
2. (c) Micro-environment
3. (d) All of these
4. (d) All of these
5. (c) Rainfall
6. (d) Sowing date
7. (d) All of these
8. (d) All of these
9. (c) Adaptation
10. (b) Adaptability
11. (b) Stability
12. (a) Specific g.a.
13. (c) Specific p.a.
14. (b) Composite variety
15. (c) Floatation rice
16. (c) Semidwarf wheat
17. (c) Synthetic variety
18. (c) (a) and (b)
19. (c) Lerner
20. (a) Finlay and Wilkinson
21. (a) 1963
22. (c) 1966
23. (d) 1971
24. (c) 1968
25. (a) Finlay and Wilkinson model
26. (d) All of these
27. (a) High
28. (d) Freeman and Perkins
29. (a) Average stability
30. (a) $b = \perp$
31. (d) Absolute stability
32. (b) Eberhart and Russell model
33. (b) Coadaptation
34. (b) Dobzhansky
35. (c) Adaptedness
36. (d) All of these
37. (a) Homeostasis
38. (d) All of these
39. (d) (b) and (c)
40. (c) Wide adaptability

FILL IN THE BLANKS

1. Comstock and Moll
2. 1963
3. Finlay and Wilkinson
4. Finlay and Wilkinson
5. 1966
6. Wheat
7. 1971
8. Freeman and Perkins
9. Eberhart and Russell
10. 1968
11. Lerner
12. 1954
13. Homeostasis
14. Balanced pulimorphism
15. Wide adaptability
16. Homeostasis
17. First order
18. Multiseason/location
19. More adaptable
20. Dobzhansky
21. 1950
22. Specific genotypic adaptation
23. Specific p.a.
24. General p.a.
25. General genotypic adaptation
26. Macro-environment
27. Micro-environment
28. Predictable factors.

TRUE OR FALSE

1. False	**2.** False	**3.** True
4. False	**5.** False	**6.** True
7. True	**8.** False	**9.** False
10. True	**11.** True	**12.** False

13. True **14.** True **15.** True
16. True **17.** False **18.** True
19. True **20.** False **21.** False
22. True.

APPROPRIATE TERM

1. Environment
2. Micro-environment
3. Macro-environment
4. Pedictable factors
5. Unpredictable factors
6. Adaptation
7. Specific genotypic adaptation
8. General g.a.
9. Specific population adaptation
10. General p.a.
11. Adaptability
12. Stability
13. Homeostasis
14. Genetic homeostasis
15. Physiological homeostasis
16. Genetic polymorphism
17. Balanced polymorphism
18. Coadaptation.

13

CHAPTER

Genetic Variances and Gene Action

A. DEFINITIONS

Gene action. The behaviour or mode of expression of genes in a genetic population. The knowledge of gene action helps in selection of suitable parents for use in the hybridization programmes and also in the choice of appropriate breeding procedure for the genetic improvement of various polygenic characters.

Genetic variance. The heritable portion of total or phenotypic variance. It is of three types, *viz.* additive, dominance and epistatic variances.

Additive variance. Average effects of genes on all segregating loci. Such genes show lack of dominance *i.e.,* intermediate expression.

Dominance variance. Deviation from the mean value due to intra allelic (single locus) interaction.

Epistatic variance. Deviation from the mean value due to non-allelic interaction *i.e.,* interaction between two or more genes (loci). It is of three types, *viz.* additive × additive, additive × dominance, and dominance × dominance.

Additive × additive epistasis. Interaction between two or more loci each exhibiting lack of dominance individually. It is denoted as AA and is fixable.

Additive × dominance epistasis. Interaction between two or more loci, one exhibiting lack of dominance and other showing dominance. It denoted as AD and is non-fixable.

Dominance × dominance epistasis. Interaction of two or more loci, each exhibiting dominance individually. It is represented as DD and is non-fixable.

Additive gene action. Additive variance plus additive × additive type of epistasis.

Non-additive gene action. Dominance variance plus two types of epistasis *viz.,* additive × dominance and dominance × dominance.

Fixable gene action. The gene action which can be fixed as a true breeding line. It includes additive gene action and additive × additive type of epistasis.

Non-fixable gene action. The gene action which can not be fixed as a true breeding line. It includes dominance gene action and additive × dominance, and dominance × dominance types of epistasis

B. BACKGROUND INFORMATION

1. Fisher (1918) divided the genetic variance into three components, *viz.,* additive, dominance and epistatic variances.
2. Wright (1935) classified genetic variance into two fractions *viz.* additive variance and non-additive variance.
3. Mather (1949) divided genetic variance into two parts, *viz.* heritable fixable and heritable non-fixable.
4. Non-additive variance includes dominance variance and epistatic variance.
5. Heritable-fixable variance includes additive variance and additive × additive (AA) type of epistasis.
6. Heritable non-fixable variance includes dominance variance and additive × dominance (AD) and dominance × dominance (DD) types of epistasis.
7. Additive variance arises from difference between two homozygotes of a gene *i.e.,* AA and aa.
8. Additive genes show lack of dominance *i.e.,* intermediate expression.
9. Additive variance is associated with homozygosity and, therefore, it is expected to be maximum in self pollinated species and minimum in cross pollinated species.
10. Additive variance is fixable and responds to selection.
11. Additive variance is used for estimation of narrow sense heritability.
12. Additive variance is a measure of breeding value of a genotype.
13. In natural plant breeding populations, additive genetic variance is predominant closely followed by dominance variance.
14. Additive gene action is the chief cause of resemblances between relatives.
15. Transgressive segregation is the result of additive gene action.
16. Transgressive segregants refer to those segregants which fall outside the range of parents.
17. Transgressive segregants are obtained due to fixation of dominant and recessive genes in separate individuals.
18. Transgressive segregants occur when parents are intermediate to the extreme values of the segregating population.
19. Dominance variance results due to interaction between alleles of the same gene or same locus. It is due to deviation of heterozygote (Aa) from the average of two homozygotes (AA and aa).

20. Dominant genes show incomplete dominance, complete dominance and overdominance.
21. Dominance variance is associated with heterozygosity and, therefore, is expected to be maximum in cross pollinated species and minimum inself pollinated species.
22. Dominance variance is non-fixable and, therefore, selection for traits governed by such variance is not effective.
23. Dominance variance is the chief cause of heterosis or hybrid vigour.
24. Dominance variance gets depleted through selfing or inbreeding.
25. In natural breeding populations, dominance variance is always lesser than additive variance.
26. Epistatic variance arises due to interaction between alleles of two or more different genes (loci).
27. Epistatic variance includes both additive and non-additive components.
28. Additive × additive type of epistasis is fixable.
29. Additive × dominance and dominance × dominance types of epistasis are non-fixable.
30. In the natural plant breeding populations, epistatic variance has the lowest magnitude.
31. Gene action is measured in terms of components of genetic variance or combining ability variances and effects.
32. Gene action is of two types *i.e.* additive gene action and non-additive gene action. Additive gene action includes additive variance and additive × additive type of epistasis.
33. Non-additive gene action includes dominance variance and additive × dominance and dominance × dominance types of epistatic variances.
34. Gene action can be studied with the help of various biometrical analysis such as diallel, partial diallel, line × tester cross, triallel, quadriallel, generation mean analysis, biparental cross and triple test cross analysis.
35. Self pollinated species have additive gene action (additive variance and additive × additive types of epistasis).
36. Cross pollinated species have both additive and non-additive gene actions (additive, dominance and epistatic variances).
37. F_2 population has ½ additive variance (½VA) and ¼ dominance variance (¼VD).
38. F_1 population has non-additive gene action (dominance and epistatic variances).
39. Random mating populations (such as composite and synthetic varieties) have both additive and non-additive gene actions.
40. Pure line selection, mass selection and progeny selection methods are used in self pollinated species having high additive gene action.
41. In cross pollinated species having additive gene action, recurrent selection for gca, synthetic and composite breeding methods are used.
42. With non-additive gene action, heterosis breeding would be rewarding both in self and cross pollinated species.
43. When a character is governed both by additive and non-additive gene actions, reciprocal recurrent selection would be rewarding for population improvement.

44. In a pure lines additive genetic variance is completely depleted and as a result further improvement through selection is not possible in a pure line population.

45. In a pure line, additive variance is regenerated over a period of time by outcrossing and mutation.

C. MULTIPLE CHOICE

1. Genetic variance refers to :
(a) Additive variance (b) Dominance variance
(c) Epistatic variance (d) All of these.

2. Intra allelic (intra locus) interaction refers to :
(a) Complete dominance (b) Incomplete dominance
(c) Over dominance (d) All of these.

3. Non-allelic interaction (interlocus interaction) refers to :
(a) Incomplete dominance (b) Complete dominance
(c) Overdominance (d) Epistasis.

4. Which of the following interactions refers to epistasis ?
(a) Additive × additive (b) Additive × dominance
(c) Dominance × dominance (d) All of these.

5. Which of the following types of epistasis is fixable ?
(a) Additive × additive (b) Additive × dominance
(c) Dominance × dominance (d) None of these.

6. Additive gene action refers to :
(a) Additive variance (b) Additive × additive epistasis
(c) (a) and (b) (d) None of these.

7. Non-additive gene action refers to :
(a) Dominance variance (b) Additive × dominance variance
(c) Dominance × dominance epistasis (d) All of these.

8. Additive type of epistasis is represented as :
(a) A × A (b) A × D
(c) D × D (d) None of these.

9. Fixable gene action includes :
(a) Additive variance (b) Additive × additive epistasis
(c) (a) and (b) (d) Additive × dominance epistasis.

10. Non-fixable gene action includes :
(a) Dominance variance (b) Additive × dominance epistasis
(c) Dominance × dominance epistatis (d) All of these.

11. Genetic variance was classified into additive, dominance and epistatic components in 1918 by :
(a) Mather (b) Fisher
(c) Hayman (d) None of these.

12. Genetic variance was divided into additive and non-additive components in 1935 by :
(a) Fisher (b) Mather
(c) Wright (d) Jinks and Jones.

13. Genetic variance was divided into heritable fixable and heritable non-fixable components in 1949 by :

(a) Mather (b) Fisher
(c) Wright (d) Hayman.

14. Fisher divided genetic variance into additive, dominance and epistatic components in :

(a) 1910 (b) 1918
(c) 1921 (d) 1936.

15. Wright divided genetic variance into additive and non additive components in :

(a) 1918 (b) 1935
(c) 1949 (d) 1954.

16. Mather divided genetic variance into heritable fixable and heritable non-fixable in :

(a) 1935 (b) 1949
(c) 1957 (d) 1962.

17. Additive genes show :

(a) Lack of dominance (b) Incomplete dominance
(c) Complete dominance (d) Overdominance.

18. Additive variance is related to :

(a) Homozygosity (b) Heritability (ns)
(c) Transgressive segregation (d) All of these.

19. Dominant genes exhibit :

(a) Incomplete dominance (b) Complete dominance
(c) Overdominance (d) All of these.

20. Dominance variance is related to :

(a) Heterozygosity (b) Out breeding
(c) Hybrid vigour (d) All of these.

21. Transgressive segregants occur from the cross involving parents with :

(a) Low value (b) Intermediate value
(c) High value (d) Very high value for a character.

22. Which of the following is predominant in the natural breeding populations ?

(a) Additive variance (b) Dominance variance
(c) Epistatic variance (d) None of these.

23. Which of the following has lowest magnitude in the natural breeding populations ?

(a) Dominance variance (b) Additive variance
(c) Epistatic variance (d) Phonotypic variance.

24. Selection is effective for traits which are governed by :

(a) Additive genes (b) Additive × additive epistasis
(c) (a) and (b) (d) Dominant genes.

25. In self pollinated species which of the following breeding methods would be effective when a character is governed by additive genes ?

(a) Pure line selection (b) Mass selection
(c) Progeny selection (d) All of these.

26. In cross pollinated species which of the following breeding methods should be used if there is preponderance of additive gene action ?

(a) Synthetic breeding (b) Composite breeding
(c) Heterosis breeding (d) (a) and (b).

27. If there is prepondence of non-additive gene action which of the following breeding method should be used :

(a) Mutation breeding (b) Heterosis breeding
(c) Line breeding (d) Backcross breeding.

28. If a trait is governed by both additive and non-additive gene actions, which of the following breeding procedures should be adopted ?

(a) Recurrent selection for gca (b) Recurrent selection for sca
(c) Reciprocal recurrent selection (d) Mass selection.

29. Selection is not effective for a trait which is governed by :

(a) Dominance variance (b) Additive × dominance epistasis
(c) Dominance × dominance epistasis (d) All of these.

30. In a pure line variety, additive variance is regenerated over a period of time due to :

(a) Outcrossing (b) Mutation
(c) Recombination (d) All of these.

D. FILL IN THE BLANKS

1. The genetic variance was divided into additive, dominance and epistatic components by ....

2. The genetic variance was grouped into additive and non-additive components by ....

3. The genetic variance was divided into heritable-fixable and heritable non-fixable by ....

4. Additive variance is heritable and ....

5. Dominance variance is heritable but ....

6. Additive variance is associated with ....

7. Additive variance has relationship with .... heritability.

8. Dominance variance is associated with ....

9. Dominance variance is the chief case of ....

10. Dominance variance is exploited for developing ....

11. Additive variance is exploited for developing ....

12. Transgression results due to .... gene action.

13. Additive × additive type of epistasis is ....

14. Dominance × dominance type of epistasis is ....

15. Additive genes exhibit ....

16. Progeny selection is effective when gene action is ....

17. Heterosis breeding is effective when gene action is .... statistics.

18. Synthetics exploit .... gene action.

19. Hybrids exploit .... gene action.
20. Intra-allelic interaction refers to ....
21. Inter-allelic interaction refers to ....
22. Selection is effective with .... variance.

E. MARK TRUE OR FALSE

1. Additive genes exhibit lack of dominance.
2. Additive variance is heritable and non-fixable.
3. Additive variance responds to selection.
4. Dominance variance is heritable and fixable.
5. Dominance variance does not respond to selection.
6. Epistatic variance in non-heritable.
7. Additive variance is required for calculation of narrow sense heritability.
8. Transgressive segregation is the result of dominance gene action.
9. Heterosis results due to dominant gene action.
10. In synthetic varieties, additive variance is exploited.
11. In hybrids, dominant gene action is exploited.
12. Inter-allelic interaction refers to dominance.
13. Intra-allelic interaction refers to epistasis.
14. In natural breeding populations, dominance variance is predominant.
15. Additive variance has the lowest magnitude in natural breeding populations.
16. F_2 population has ½ additive variance (½VA).
17. F_2 population had ¼ dominance variance (¼VD).
18. Additive × additive type of epistasis is nonfixable .
19. Dominance × dominance type of epistasis is fixable.
20. Dominance variance is the chief cause of heterosis.
21. Additive gene action is the chief cause of resemblances between relatives.
22. Self pollinated species have non-additive gene action.

F. USE APPROPRIATE TERM

1. The mode of expression of genes in a genetic population.
2. The heritable portion of phenotypic variance.
3. Average effects of genes on all segregating loci.
4. Deviation from the mean value due to intra-allelic interaction.
5. Deviation from the mean value due to intra-allelic interaction.
6. Interaction between two or more loci each exhibiting lack of dominance individually.
7. Interaction between two loci, one exhibiting lack of dominance and other showing dominance.
8. Interaction between two loci, each exhibiting dominance individually.
9. The gene action which can be fixed as a true breeding line.
10. The gene action which cannot be fixed as a true breeding line

ANSWERS

MULTIPLE CHOICE

1. (d) All of these
2. (d) All of these
3. (d) Epistasis
4. (d) All of these
5. (a) Additive × additive
6. (c) (a) and (b)
7. (d) All of these
8. (a) A × A
9. (c) (a) and (b)
10. (d) All of these
11. (b) Fisher
12. (c) Wright
13. (a) Mather
14. (b) 1918
15. (b) 1935
16. (b) 1949
17. (a) Lack of dominance
18. (d) All of these
19. (d) All of these
20. (d) All of these
21. (b) Intermediate value
22. (a) Additive variance
23. (c) Epistatic variance
24. (c) (a) and (b)
25. (d) All of these
26. (d) (a) and (b)
27. (b) Heterosis breeding
28. (c) Reciprocal RS
29. (d) All of these
30. (d) All of these

FILL IN THE BLANKS

1. Fisher
2. Wright
3. Mather
4. Fixable
5. Non-fixable
6. Homozygosity
7. Narrow sense
8. Heterozygosity
9. Heterosis
10. Hybrids
11. Synthetics
12. Additive
13. Fixable
14. Non-fixable
15. Lack of dominance
16. Additive
17. Non-additive
18. Additive
19. Non-additive
20. Dominance
21. Epistasis
22. Additive

TRUE OR FALSE

1. True	2. False	3. True
4. False	5. True	6. False
7. True	8. True	9. True
10. True	11. True	12. False
13. False	14. False	15. False
16. True	17. True	18. False
19. False	20. True	21. True
22. False.		

APPROPRIATE TERM

1. Gene action
2. Genetic variance
3. Additive variance
4. Dominance variance
5. Epistatic variance
6. Additive × additive epistasis
7. Additive × dominance epistasis
8. Dominance × dominance epistasis
9. Fixable gene action
10. Non-fixable gene action

●●●

14

CHAPTER

Heritability and Genetic Advance

A. DEFINITIONS

Heritability. The ratio genotypic variance to the phenotypic variance expressed in percentage. Heritability is estimated in two ways, *viz.* in broad sence and in narrow sense.

Broad sense heritability. Ratio of total genetic variance to the phenotypic variance. Total genetic variance includes additive, dominance and epistatic variances.

Narrow sense heritability. Ratio of additive genetic variance to the phenotypic variance.

Coheritability. Ratio of genotypic covariance to the phenotypic covariance. It measures simultaneous inheritance of two characters.

Repeatability. Estimation of the ratio of genotypic variance to the phenotypic variance from a biased sample (non random sample) of genotypes. This does not provide true estimates of heritability.

Genetic advance. Improvement in the mean genotypic value of selected plants over the parental population. It is the measure of genetic gain under selection. Genetic advance is calculated as follows :

$$\text{Genetic advance} = \frac{Vg}{VP} \times \sqrt{VP} \times K$$

where V*g* = genotypic variance, VP = phenotypic variance and K = selection differential (a constant *i.e.* 2.06).

Genetic gain. The difference between the mean phenotypic value of the progeny of selected plants and the base population. Genetic gain is denoted by R which is estimated as follows.

$$R = \bar{X}P - \bar{X}O$$

where $\overline{X}P$ = mean phenotypic value of the progeny of selected plants, XO = mean value of base population.

Selection differential. Different between the mean phenotypic value of selected plants and mean phenotypic value of parental population.

Selection Intensity. The proportion of plants or families selected from a genetic population for study.

B. BACKGROUND INFORMATION

1. Heritability is an index of the transmission of characters from parents to their offspring.
2. Estimates of heritability help plant breeders in selection of elite genotypes from diverse genetic populations.
3. Broad sense heritability can be estimated from both parental as well as segregating populations.
4. Broad sense heritability is estimated from total genetic variance.
5. Broad sense heritability is more useful in animal breeding than in plant breeding.
6. Broad sense heritability is useful in selection of elite genotypes from homozygous material.
7. Broad sense heritability is estimated using following formula.

   Heritability $(bs) = \frac{Vg}{Vp} \times 100$ where Vg = genotypic variance and Vp = phenotypic variance.
8. For estimation of narrow sense heritability, crosses have to be made in a definite fashion.
9. Narrow sense heritability is estimated from additive genetic variance.
10. Narrow sense heritability is useful both in plant and animal breeding.
11. Narrow sense heritability is useful in selecting elite types from segregating populations.
12. Narrow sense heritability is estimated as follows.

    Heritability $(ns) = \frac{\frac{1}{2}D}{Vp}$, where D is the additive genetic variance and Vp = phenotypic variance.
13. Coheritability measures inheritance of two characters simultaneously.
14. Estimates of coheritability are useful in simultaneous improvement of two characters.
15. Coheritability is estimated with the help of following formula

    Coheritability $(X_1, X_2) = \frac{G\,Cov\,X_1X_2}{P\,Cov\,X_1X_2} \times 100$ where G Cov and P Cov are genotypic and phenotypic covariance between characters X_1 and X_2.
16. High values of coheritability estimates suggest that increase in one polygenic trait will lead to simultaneous increase in another coheritable character.

17. Genetic advance is the measure of genetic gain under selection.

18. The success of genetic advance under selection depends on three main factors, *viz.* genetic variability, heritability and selection intensity.

19. Estimates of heritability and genetic advance are free from genetical assumptions.

20. Linkage influences the heritability estimates by causing an upward or downward bias in the estimates of additive and dominance variances.

21. High frequency of coupling phase linkage (AB/*ab*) cause an upward bias in the estimates of additive and dominance variances.

22. Warner (1952) suggested the following formula for estimating heritability in narrow sense from generation mean analysis.

Heritability (*ns*) $\frac{\frac{1}{2}D}{VF_2} \times 100$ where D and VF_2 are additive and phenotypic variance, respectively.

23. Mather (1949) suggested the following formula for estimation of heritability (*ns*) from generation mean analysis.

$$\text{Heritability } (ns) \ \frac{D}{D+H+E} = \times 100$$

Where D, H and E are additive, non additive and error variance respectively.

24. Verhalen and Murray (1969) proposed the following formula for calculation of heritability from F_2 generation of diallel cross.

$$\text{Heritability } (ns) = \frac{\frac{1}{4}D}{\frac{1}{4}D + \frac{1}{16}H_1 - \frac{1}{8}F + E} \times 100$$

25. From diallel cross, the heritability can be calculated by the following formula

$$\text{Heritability } (ns) = \frac{\frac{1}{2}D + \frac{1}{2}H_1 - \frac{1}{2}H_2 - \frac{1}{2}F}{\frac{1}{2}D + \frac{1}{2}H_1 - \frac{1}{2}H_2 - \frac{1}{2}F + E} \times 100.$$

26. If the value of genetic advance is high, it indicates that the character is governed by additive genes.

27. If the value of genetic advance is low, it indicates that the character is governed by non-additive genes.

28. If the heritability estimates are high in narrow sense, it means the character is largely governed by additive genes and selection for improvement of such character would be rewarding.

29. Low estimates of narrow sense heritability are indicative on non-additive gene action.

30. High heritability with high genetic advance is indicative of additive gene effects.

31. High heritability with low genetic advance is indicative of non-additive gene action.

32. It is not necessary that a character showing high heritability will also exhibit high genetic advance.

C. MULTIPLE CHOICES

1. The ratio of genotypic variance to phenotypic variance refers to :
   (a) Broad sense heritability (b) Narrow sense heritability
   (c) (a) and (b) above (d) None of these.

2. The ratio of additive variance to phenotypic variance refers to :
   (a) Broad sense heritability (b) Narrow sense heritability
   (c) Coheritability (d) Repeatability.

3. Genotypic variance includes :
   (a) Additive variance (b) Dominance variance
   (c) Epistatic variance (d) All of these.

4. The ratio of genotypic variance to phenotypic variance from a biased sample is called :
   (a) Coheritability (b) Repeatability
   (c) Heritability (*bs*) (d) Heritability (*ns*).

5. The formula $\frac{Vg}{VP} \times \sqrt{VP} \times K$ is used for calculation of :
   (a) Genetic gain (b) Genetic advance
   (c) Selection differential (d) Selection intensity.

6. The formula $\frac{Vg}{Vp} \times 100$ is used for calculation of :
   (a) Heritability (*bs*) (b) Heritability (*ns*)
   (c) Genetic advance (d) None of these.

7. The formula $\frac{\frac{1}{2}D}{VP} \times 100$ is used for estimation of :
   (a) Coheritability (b) Heritability (*ns*)
   (c) Heritability (*bs*) (d) Genetic advance.

8. The formula $\frac{G\,Cov\,X_1X_2}{P\,Cov\,X_1X_2} \times 100$ is used for calculation of :
   (a) Combining ability (b) Repeatability
   (c) Coheritability (d) None of these.

9. The formula $\frac{\frac{1}{2}D}{VF_2} \times 100$ was proposed for calculation of heritability (*ns*) by :
   (a) Mather (b) Falconer
   (c) Warner (d) None of these.

10. The formula $\frac{\frac{1}{2}D}{VF_2} \times 100$ is used for calculation of heritability from :
    (a) Diallel cross (b) Partial diallel cross
    (c) Line × tester cross (d) Generation means.

11. Warner proposed the formula $\frac{\frac{1}{2}D}{VF_2} \times 100$ for calculation of heritability from generation means in :

(a) 1921 (b) 1936
(c) 1952 (d) 1981.

12. The formula $\frac{D}{D+H+E} \times 100$ was proposed for calculation of heritability in 1949 by :

(a) Hayman (b) Warner
(c) Mather (d) Jinks and Jones.

13. The formula $\frac{D}{D+H+E} \times 100$ is used for calculation of heritability (*ns*) from :

(a) Biparental cross (b) Generation means
(c) Triple test cross (d) Diallel cross.

14. The formula $\frac{\frac{1}{4}D}{\frac{1}{4}D+\frac{1}{16}H_1-\frac{1}{8}F+E} \times 100$ was proposed for estimation of heritability in 1969 by :

(a) Mather and Jinks (b) Hayman and Jinks
(c) Verhalen and Murray (d) Jinks and Jones.

15. The above formula was proposed for calculation of heritability from :

(a) Diallel cross (F_2) (b) Diallel cross (F_1)
(c) Generation means (d) Line × tester cross.

16. Verhalen and Murray proposed the above formula (Item 14) for calculation of heritability (*ns*) in :

(a) 1947 (b) 1954
(c) 1969 (d) 1981.

17. The formula $\frac{\frac{1}{2}D+\frac{1}{2}H_1-\frac{1}{2}H_2-\frac{1}{2}F}{\frac{1}{2}D+\frac{1}{2}H_1-\frac{1}{2}H_2-\frac{1}{2}F+E} \times 100$ is used for calculation of heritability from :

(a) Diallel cross (F_1) (b) Diallel cross (F_2)
(c) Partial diallel (d) Generation means.

18. The success of genetic advance under selection for a character depends on :

(a) Genetic variability (b) Heritibility of a character
(c) Selection intensity (d) All of these.

19. Coupling phase linkage leads to an upward bias in the estimates of :

(a) Additive variance (b) Dominance variance
(c) (a) and (b) (d) Epistatic variance.

20. High value of genetic advance indicates that the character is governed by :
(a) Additive genes (b) Dominant genes
(c) Epistatic genes (d) All of these.

21. Low value of genetic advance is indicative of :
(a) Additive genes (b) Non-additive genes
(c) Epistatic genes (d) (a) and (b).

22. High estimates of narrow sense heritability are indicative of :
(a) Additive gene action (b) Dominance gene action
(c) Epistatic variance (d) None of these.

23. Low estimates (values) of narrow sense heritability are indicative of :
(a) Additive gene action (b) Non-additive gene action
(c) Epistasis (d) None of these.

24. High heritability with high genetic advance is indicative of :
(a) Additive gene action (b) Dominance action
(c) Non-additive gene action (d) Epistatic gene action.

25. High heritability with low genetic advance is indicative of :
(a) Epistatic gene action (b) Dominance gene action
(c) Non-additive gene action (d) Additive gene action.

26. The difference between mean phenotypic value of the progony of selected plants and original population is called :
(a) Genetic advance (b) Genetic gain
(c) Selection differential (d) None of the above.

27. Repeatability estimates are obtained from :
(a) Random sample (b) Biased sample
(c) Stratified sample (d) None of these.

28. The selection differential is represented as :
(a) R (b) K
(c) Q (d) Z.

D. FILL IN THE BLANKS

1. The ratio of genotypic variance to phenotypic variance refers to ....
2. Broad sense heritability is estimated from .... genetic variance.
3. Narrow sense heritability is estimated from .... genetic variance.
4. Heritability measures inheritance of .... character.
5. Coheritability measures inheritance of .... characters.
6. The formula $\frac{Vg}{VP} \times \sqrt{VP} \times K$ is used for estimation of ....
7. The formula $R = \overline{X}P - \overline{X}O$ is used for estimation of ....
8. The formula $\frac{VG}{VP} \times 100$ is used for estimation of ....

9. The formula $\frac{\frac{1}{2}D}{VP} \times 100$ is used for estimation of ....

10. The formula $\frac{D}{D+H+E} \times 100$ is used for estimation of ....

11. The above formula of estimating heritability was proposed by ....

12. Mather proposed the above formula of estimating heritability in ....

13. The formula $\frac{\frac{1}{2}D}{VF_2} \times 100$ was proposed for estimating heritability by ....

14. The formula $\frac{\frac{1}{2}D}{VF_2} \times 100$ is used for estimating ....

15. The formula $\frac{\frac{1}{4}D}{\frac{1}{4}D+\frac{1}{16}H_1-\frac{1}{8}F+E} \times 100$ of estimating heritability was proposed by ....

16. Above formula is used to estimate heritability from .... of a diallel cross

17. High value of genetic advance are indicative of .... gene action.

18. Low value of genetic advance is indicative of .... gene action.

19. High value of heritability (*ns*) is indicative of .... gene action.

20. High values of genetic advance and heritability are indicate of .... gene action.

21. High heritability with low genetic advance indicate .... gene action.

22. Low value of *ns* heritability is indicative of .... gene action.

E. MARK TRUE OR FALSE

1. Heritability is the index of transmission of characters from parents to their offspring.

2. Heritability is the ratio of phenotypic variance to genotypic variance.

3. Additive variance is required for estimation of broad sense heritability.

4. Estimation of narrow sense heritability is based on total genetic variance.

5. Heritability measures inheritance of two characters.

6. Coheritability measures inheritance of single character.

7. The formula $\frac{VG}{VP} \times 100$ is used for estimation of broad sense heritability.

8. The formula $\frac{\frac{1}{2}D}{VP} \times 100$ is used for estimation of narrow sense heritability.

9. Broad sense heritability is useful in selection of elite genotypes from homozygous material.

10. Narrow sense heritability is useful in selecting elite types from segregating populations.

11. The formula $\frac{\frac{1}{2}D}{VF_2} \times 100$ was proposed by Mather for estimation of narrow sense heritability.

12. The formula $\frac{D}{D+H+E} \times 100$ was proposed by Warner.

13. The method of calculating heritability from F_2 generation of a diallel cross was given by Verhalen and Murray.

14. High value of heritability (*ns*) is indicative of non-additive gene action.

15. High value of genetic advance is indicative of additive gene action.

16. Estimates of heritability are free from genetical assumptions.

17. High value of heritability and high genetic advance indicate non-additive gene action.

18. Low value of heritability and low genetic advance indicate additive gene action.

19. The formula $\frac{VG}{VP} \times \sqrt{VP} \times K$ is used for estimation of genetic advance.

20. The heritability estimates are influenced by linkage

F. USE APPROPRIATE TERM

1. The ratio of genotypic variance to phenotypic variance.
2. The ratio of total genetic variance to phenotypic variance.
3. The ratio of additive variance to phenotypic variance.
4. The ratio of genotypic covariance to phenotypic covariance.
5. Estimation of heritability from a biased sample.
6. Improvement in the mean genotypic value of selected plants over the parent population.
7. The difference between the mean phenotypic value of the progeny of selected plants and the base population.
8. Difference between the mean phenotypic value of the selected plants and mean phenotypic value of parental population.
9. The proportion of plants or families selected from a genetic population for study.

ANSWERS

MULTIPLE CHOICE

1. (a) Heritability (*bs*)
2. (b) Heritability (*ns*)
3. (d) All of these
4. (b) Repeatability
5. (b) Genetic advance
6. (b) Heritability (*bs*)
7. (b) Heritability (*ns*)
8. (c) Coheritability
9. (c) Warner

10. (d) Generation means
11. (c) 1952
12. (c) Mather
13. (b) Generation means
14. (c) Verhalen and Murray
15. (a) F_2 diallel cross
16. (c) 1969
17. (a) F_1 diallel cross
18. (d) All of these
19. (c) (a) and (b)
20. (a) Additive genes
21. (b) Non-additive genes
22. (a) Additive gene action
23. (b) Non-additive gene action
24. (a) Additive gene action
25. (c) Non-additive gene action
26. (b) Genetic gain
27. (b) Biased sample
28. (b) K

FILL IN THE BLANKS

1. Heritability
2. Toal
3. Additive
4. Single or one
5. Two
6. Genetic advance
7. Genetic gain
8. Heritability (*bs*)
9. Heritability (*ns*)
10. Heritability (*ns*)
11. Mather
12. Narrow sense
13. Warner
14. Heritability (*ns*)
15. Verhalen and Murray
16. F_2 generation
17. Additive
18. Non-additive
19. Additive
20. Additive
21. Non-additive
22. Non-additive

TRUE OR FALSE

1. True	2. False	3. True
4. True	5. False	6. False
7. True	8. True	9. True
10. True	11. False	12. False
13. True	14. False	15. True
16. True	17. False	18. False
19. True	20. True.	

APPROPRIATE TERM

1. Heritability
2. Heritability (*bs*)
3. Heritability (*ns*)
4. Coheritability
5. Repeatability
6. Genetic advance
7. Genetic gain
8. Selection differential
9. Selection intensity

●●●

15

CHAPTER

Combining Ability

A. DEFINITIONS

Combining ability. The capacity of a genotype to transmit superior performance to its crosses. It is of two types, *viz.* general combining ability and specific combining ability. Combining ability is a measure of gene action.

General combining ability. Average performance of a genotype in a series of hybrid combinations. It is a measure of additive gene action. General combining ability is primarily a function of additive variance and additive epistasis.

Specific combining ability. The performance of a genotype (parent) in a specific cross in relation to general combining ability. It is a measure of non-additive gene action. sca is primarily a function of dominance variance and two types of epistasis, *viz.* additive × dominance and dominance × dominance.

Gene action. The mode of expression of genes in a genetic population.

Additive gene action. Joint effects of additive variance plus additive × additive type of epistasis.

Non-additive gene action. Joint effect of dominance and additive × dominance and dominance × dominance types of epistasis.

B. BACKGROUND INFORMATION

1. The concept of combining ability as a measure of gene action was first proposed by Sprague and Tatum in 1942 working with maize.
2. Combining ability analysis is useful in identification of good general combiners and superior hybrid combinations.
3. Combining ability analysis provides information about the gene action involved in the expression of various polygenic characters and thus helps in deciding the suitable breeding procedure for genetic improvement of such traits.

4. Combining ability analysis is carried out by diallel, partial diallel and line × tester cross techniques.
5. The gca is primarily due to additive variance, but if epistases is present it will also include additive × additive of epistasis.
6. The general combining ability (gca) is estimated from half sib families.
7. The gca variance has positive correlation with narrow sense heritability.
8. The estimates of gca help in identification of good general combing parents for hybridization.
9. The specific combining ability (sca) is mainly due to dominance variance, but if epistasis is present, it will also include additive × dominance and dominance × dominance type of epistasis.
10. The sca is estimated from full sib families.
11. The sca variance has positive association with heterosis of hybrid vigour.
12. The sca estimates help in identification of superior cross combinations for development of commercial hybrids.
13. If gca variance is higher than sca variance, it indicates preponderance of additive gene action.
14. If sca variance is higher than gca variance, it indicates preponderance of non-additive gene action.
15. If gca and sca variances are of equal magnitude, it suggests that additive and non-additive genes are equally important for the expression of character.
16. If there is preponderance of additive gene action, progeny selection will be effective for genetic improvement of such character.
17. When there is preponderance of additive gene action, heterosis breeding would be rewarding.
18. When additive and non-additive gene actions are of equal magnitude, reciprocal recurrent selection may be used for population improvement.
19. Combining ability analysis requires specific mating design.
20. The existence of significant amount of dominance variance is a pre-requisite for the exploitation of heterosis.
21. Estimates of combining ability effects are based on first order statistics.
22. Combining ability estimates are free from genetical assumptions.

C. MULTIPLE CHOICE

1. The concept of combining ability analysis was first proposed in 1942 by :

   (a) Wright (b) Hayman
   (c) Sprague and Tatum (d) Jinks and Jones.

2. The use of combining ability as a measure of gene action was first suggested by :

   (a) Hayman (b) Griffing
   (c) Sprague and Tatum (d) None of these.

3. Sprague and Tatum proposed combining ability analysis in :
   (a) 1936 (b) 1942
   (c) 1954 (d) 1957.
4. Sprague and Tatum developed the concept of combining ability analysis working with :
   (a) Garden pea (b) Maize
   (c) Sorghum (d) Pearl millet.
5. Combining ability analysis provides information about :
   (a) Linkage (b) Pleiotropy
   (c) Gene action (d) All of these.
6. The gca variance includes :
   (a) Additive variance (b) Additive × additive epistatsis
   (c) (a) and (b) (d) Dominance variance.
7. The sca variance includes :
   (a) Dominance variance (b) Additive × dominance epistasis
   (c) Dominance × dominance (d) All of these.
8. The gca is estimated from :
   (a) Half sib crosses (b) Full sib crosses
   (c) (a) and (b) above (d) None of these.
9. The combining ability analysis is done using :
   (a) Diallel cross (b) Partial diallel cross
   (c) Line × tester cross (d) All of these.
10. Which breeding method would be rewarding, when there is preponderance of additive gene action :
   (a) Heterosis breeding (b) Progeny selection
   (c) Simple recurrent selection (d) None of these.
11. Which breeding method would be effective when there is preponderance of non-additive gene actions ?
   (a) Progeny selection (b) Reciprocal recurrent selection
   (c) Heterosis breeding (d) All of these.
12. When there is equal magnitude of additive and non-additive gene actions, which of the following breeding methods would be effective :
   (a) Reciprocal recurrent selection (b) Progeny selection
   (c) Heterosis breeding (d) Line breeding.
13. Higher value of gca than sca indicates preponderance of :
   (a) Dominance (b) Epistasis
   (c) Additive genes (d) Linkage.
14. Higher value of sca variance than gca variance reveals preponderance of :
   (a) Additive gene action (b) Non-additive gene action
   (c) (a) and (b) above (d) Lethal genes.
15. Combining ability analysis provides information about :
   (a) Gene action (b) Good general combiners
   (c) Good specific combinations (d) All of these.

16. Additive gene action refers to :

(a) Additive variance
(b) Additive × additive epistasis
(c) (a) and (b)
(d) Dominance variance.

17. Non-additive gene action refers to :

(a) Dominance variance
(b) Additive × dominance epistasis
(c) Dominance × dominance epistasis
(d) All of these.

18. The gca variance has positive association with :

(a) Narrow sense heritability
(b) Adaptability
(c) Hybrid vigour
(d) All of these.

19. The sca variance has positive association with :

(a) Adaptability
(b) Heterosis
(c) Linkage
(d) Heritability (*ns*)

20. Estimates of combining ability effects involve statistics of :

(a) First order
(b) Second order
(c) Third order
(d) (a) and (b) above.

D. FILL IN THE BLANKS

1. Combining ability as a measure of gene action was first proposed by ....
2. Sprague and Tatum proposed combining ability as a measure of gene action in ....
3. Sprague and Tatum coined the term Combining ability working with .... crop.
4. Estimates of combining ability (ca) effects are based on .... statistics.
5. General combining ability (gca) is estimated from .... families.
6. Specific combining ability (sca) is estimated from .... families.
7. High values of gca are indicative of .... gene action.
8. High values of sca are indicative of .... gene action.
9. gca variance has positive association with .... heritability.
10. sca variance has positive association with ....
11. The gca is primarily due to .... variance.
12. The sca is mainly due to .... variance.
13. Progeny selection is effective when there is preponderance of .... gene action.
14. Heterosis breeding is rewarding when there is preponderance of ....gene action.
15. When additive and non-additive gene actions are of equal magnitude .... selection would be rewarding.
16. Combining ability analysis provides information about ....
17. Additive × additive epistasis is ....
18. Dominance × dominance type of epistasis is ....
19. The concept of gca is used in developing .... varieties.
20. The concept of sca is used in developing .... varieties

E. MARK TRUE OR FALSE

1. The concept of combining ability analysis was developed by Wright.
2. The combining ability is a measure of gene action.
3. Combining ability analysis is based on genetical assumptions.
4. gca is mainly due to non-additive variance.
5. sca is mainly the function of additive variance.
6. gca is estimated from full sub families.
7. sca is estimated from sub families.
8. High value of gca are indicative of additive gene action.
9. High values of sca are indicative of non-additive gene action.
10. Additive genetic variance responds to selection.
11. Non-additive variance does not respond to selection.
12. Additive × additive type of epistasis is non-fixable.
13. Dominance × dominance type of epistasis is fixable.
14. Estimates of combining ability effects are based on first order statistics.
15. sca variance has positive association with heteroses.
16. gca variance has positive association with narrow sense heritability.
17. The concept of gca is exploited in developing hybrid varieties.
18. The concept of sca is exploited in developing hybrid varieties.
19. gca helps in identification of good general combiners.
20. sca helps in identification of superior hybrid combinations.

F. USE APPROPRIATE TERM

1. The capacity of a genotype to transmit superior performance to its crosses.
2. Average performance of a genotype in a series of hybrid combinations.
3. The performance of a genotype in a specific cross in relation to general combining ability.
4. The mode of expression of genes in a genetic population.
5. The heritable and fixable types of variance.
6. The heritable but non-fixable type of variance.

ANSWERS

MULTIPLE CHOICE

1. (c) Sprague and Tatum
2. (c) Sprague and Tatum
3. (b) 1942
4. (b) Maize
5. (c) Gene action
6. (c) (a) and (b)
7. (d) All of these
8. (a) Half sib crosses
9. (d) All of these
10. (b) Progeny selection
11. (c) Heterosis breeding

12. (a) Reciprocal RS
13. (c) Additive genes
14. (b) Non-additive gene action
15. (d) All of these
16. (c) (a) and (b)
17. (d) All of these
18. (a) *ns* heritability
19. (b) Heterosis
20. (a) First order

FILL IN THE BLANKS

1. Sprague and Tatum
2. 1942
3. Maize
4. First order
5. Half sib
6. Full sib
7. Additive
8. Non-additive
9. Narrow sense
10. Heterosis
11. Additive
12. Non-additive
13. Additive
14. Non-additive
15. Reciprocal recurrent
16. Gene action
17. Fixable
18. Non-fixable
19. Synthetic
20. Hybrid

TRUE OR FALSE

1. False	2. True	3. False
4. False	5. False	6. False
7. False	8. True	9. True
10. True	11. True	12. False
13. False	14. True	15. True
16. True	17. False	18. False
19. True	20. True.	

APPROPRIATE TERM

1. Combining ability
2. gca
3. sca
4. Gene action
5. Additive variance
6. Non-additive variance

16 CHAPTER

Breeding Value

A. DEFINITIONS

Breeding value. The genetic worth of an individual that is transmitted to its offspring.

Genotypic value. The value of an individual or character associated with a genotype.

Phenotypic value. The value of a character as determined by the genotype (genotypic value) and environmental interaction.

Practical breeding value. Measurement of the breeding value from the mean of its progeny.

Theoretical breeding value. The sum of average effects of genes over all loci or sum of average effects of alleles of an individual.

B. BACKGROUND INFORMATION

1. Breeding value is defined as the genetic worth (genetic quality) of an individual which is transmitted to the offspring.
2. Breeding value is useful in both animal breeding as well as plant breeding. However, it is commonly used in animal breeding than in plant breeding.
3. Estimates of breeding value give an idea about the transmitting ability of the parent. In other words, it expresses the value transmitted from the parents to their offspring.
4. The breeding value of an individual is measured from the mean performance of its progeny. In other words, breeding value of an individual is defined as the mean performance of its progeny.
5. Breeding values of parents predict the performance of their offspring. In other words, breeding value provide a measure of the performance expected from the offspring of an individual.

6. Breeding value is an important measure of the genetic quality of the available material. In other words, it refers to genetic worth of an individual. The genetic worth is the measure of the genetic quality on an individual.

7. Breeding values are calculated for specific trait or for an individual. In plant breeding and genetics, breeding values of parents are calculated for yield, quality, earliness, resistance to biotic and abiotic stresses, etc.

8. The estimates of breeding value are specific to the genetic material and environment in which the material has been tested.

9. Breeding values are estimated from phenotypic observations recorded on different traits of an individual. Breeding value is the property of the individual and the population from which its mates (parents) are selected.

10. The breeding value of an individual is expressed in two ways, *viz.* (*i*) practical breeding value, and (*ii*) theoretical breeding value. These are explained as follows.

11. When the breeding value of an individual is measured by the mean of its progeny, it is referred to as practical breeding value. This method is widely used for calculating of breeding value in both animal breeding and plant breeding. The main features of practical breeding value are given below :

    (i) It is calculated as the mean value of the progeny of an individual.

    (ii) It is widely used in animal breeding.

    (iii) It is expressed in the form of deviation from population mean.

    (iv) If an individual is mated with a random sample of individuals from a population, its breeding value for a given trait is twice the mean deviation of the progeny from the population mean. It is because the progeny receive half the genes from the parent and other half genes from the random population.

    (v) The value of a character as determined by the genotype (genotypic value) and environmental interaction.

    (vi) The expected values are mean values of large number of offspring of the same parent. In other words, the expected breeding value of any individual is the mean of the breeding values of its two parents.

12. In quantitative genetics, breeding value of an individual is defined as the sum of average effects of genes over all loci. For a single locus with two alleles, the breeding of the genotypes are as follows.

    Using Deviation *d*1 A1 = 10 and *d*2 A2 = – 10

    (i) Breeding value of genotype A1A1 = 10 + 10 = 20

    (ii) Breeding value of genotype A1A2 = 10 – 10 = 0

    (iii) Breeding value of genotype A2A2 = – 10 – 10 = – 20

    Main points related to theoretical breeding value as listed below :

    (a) It is calculated as sum of average effects of alleles of an individual.

    (b) The additive genetic effects of an individual are passed on to the progeny. Hence, additive genetic effect is also referred to as breeding value.

    (c) Non-additive effects and environmental effects cannot be passed to the progeny. Hence, such effects are not used for calculation of breeding value.

(d) The breeding value is sometimes referred to as the additive genotype and variation in breeding value is ascribed to the additive effects of genes.

13. Breeding value of an individual is expressed by the numerical difference of its offspring from the population mean. This value directly predicts genetic gain and the value of its progeny.

14. Genotypic Value is defined as the value of an individual or trait associated with a genotype. It is measured in terms of phenotype of a genotype.

15. Phenotypic Value is defined as the value of a character as determined by the genotype (genetic value) and environment (environmental deviation).

16. Genetic Value refers to the value of genes to the individual itself. It is measured from additive gene effects. It is calculated from the performance of an individual. It helps in selection of an individual.

17. Breeding Value refers to the value of genes to its progeny. It involves both additive and non-additive gene effects. It is calculated from the mean performance of progeny. It helps in selection of parents.

18. In plant breeding, there are two broad methods of estimating breeding value of an individual, *viz.* biometrical techniques and molecular techniques. Various estimates that provide information about genetic worth of an individual include mean deviation, regression analysis, heritability and combining ability. Various biometrical techniques such as diallel cross, partial diallel cross, line × tester cross, triple test cross, biparental cross and generation mean analyses are commonly used for evaluating the genetic worth of various genotypes.

19. Various molecular technique that are used to find out the genetic worth of an individual include RFLP, AFLP, RAPD, CAPS, SSR, SNP, etc.

20. The breeding value differs from individual to individual and trait to trait. All individuals and all traits cannot have the same breeding value. The genetic constitution of each progeny is different due to difference in the alleles received from two parents. In crop plants, the important measures of breeding value prepotency, heritability, parent offspring regression, combining ability, mean deviation, and genetic advance.

21. The genetic superiority of an individual for a specific trait is determined by its genetic make-up or its genotype. The value of a genotype is determined by the value genes it carries and by the interactions between the genes. The genotypic value can only be assessed by measuring the phenotypes. The phenotypic variation consists of genotypic and environmental variations and genotypic variation consists of additive variance, and non-additive variance. It can be represented as follows.

$$VP = VG + VE$$

$$VG = VA + VNA$$

or

$$VP = VA + VNA + VE$$

Thus, breeding value of an individual is also determined by the environment where the progeny is grown.

Thus, breeding values are also specific to genetic material and the environmental conditions.

22. A genetically superior individual is not necessarily a genetically superior parent. A parent passes on its genes but not its genotype to its progeny. The mean value of the progeny of a parent is used to determine its genetic superiority as a parent.

23. The breeding value of an individual is influenced by several factors. Such factors include genetic material, gene effects, mode of inheritance, sample size, sampling method and method of calculation.

24. Breeding values of parents are useful; in several ways in plant breeding, animal breeding and tree breeding as discussed below :

(i) In crop improvement programs, breeding values are used in the selection of suitable parents in the hybridization programs for developing superior cultivars.

(ii) Breeding values are also used in the choice of breeding procedures for genetic improvement of various polygenic traits.

(iii) Breeding values of parents are useful in predicting the performance of their offspring.

(iv) Breeding values are also useful in making decisions for the selection of advanced generation breeding population.

(v) In tree breeding, (forest breeding), breeding values are useful in the selection of superior stocks of timber trees.

(vi) In animal breeding, breeding values are used for selection of superior sire and dam for beef and milk production.

25. The breeding value has some limitations or demerits which are listed below :

(i) The breeding value is specific to the genetic material and environmental conditions. It is estimated in terms of phenotype which varies under different environmental conditions. In other words, breeding value is the property of an individual and the population from which its mates (parents) have been selected.

(ii) The estimates of breeding value vary according to the method of calculation.

(iii) In tree breeding, the progeny performance is estimated at younger than actual age of harvest of timber trees. It leads to uncertainty about the reliability of breeding value.

(iv) In crop breeding, it sometimes become impossible to measure all the progeny of a parent. Moreover, it is also impossible to test the material under all environmental conditions.

C. MULTIPLE CHOICE

1. Breeding value is useful in :

(a) Plant breeding (b) Animal breeding
(c) Tree breeding (d) All of these.

2. Breeding value is more commonly used in :

(a) Plant breeding (b) Animal breeding
(c) Tree breeding (d) All of these.

3. Breeding value is useful in :

(a) Plant breeding (b) Animal breeding
(c) Tree breeding (d) All of these.

4. Breeding values of parents are calculated for :
(a) Yield (b) Quality
(c) Earliness (d) All of these.

5. The breeding value of an individual is influenced by :
(a) Genetic material (b) Gene effects
(c) Mode of inheritance (d) All of these.

6. The breeding value of an individual is influenced by :
(a) Sample size (b) Sampling method
(c) Method of calculation (d) All of these.

7. Phenotypic variation consists of :
(a) Genotypic variation (b) Environmental variation
(c) Both (a) and (b) (d) None of these.

8. Genotypic variation consists of :
(a) Additive variation (b) Dominance variation
(c) Epistatic variation (d) All of these.

9. Which of the following is heritable ?
(a) Additive variation (b) Dominance variation
(c) Epistatic variation (d) All of these.

10. Which of the following techniques is used for estimation of breeding value ?
(a) Diallel cross (b) Partial diallel cross
(c) Line × tester cross (d) All of these.

11. Which of the following techniques is used for estimation of breeding value ?
(a) Triple test cross (b) Biparental cross
(c) Triallel cross (d) All of these.

12. Which of the following techniques is used for estimation of breeding value ?
(a) Quadriallel cross (b) Heritability
(c) Generation means (d) All of these.

13. Which of the following techniques is used for estimation of breeding value ?
(a) Mean deviation (b) Regression analysis
(c) Combining ability (d) All of these.

14. Breeding value is related to :
(a) Additive variance (b) Dominance variance
(c) Epistatic variance (d) All of these.

D. FILL IN THE BLANKS

1. Breeding value is defined as the genetic .... of an individual.

2. Breeding value expresses the value transmitted from the parents to their ....

3. The breeding value of an individual is measured from the mean performance of its ....

4. Breeding values of parents predict the performance of their ....

5. The genetic worth is the measure of the genetic .... of an individual.

6. Breeding values are calculated for specific .... or for an individual.
7. Measurement of the breeding value from the mean of its progeny ....
8. The sum of average effects of genes over all loci or sum of average effects of alleles of an individual refers to ....
9. The value of an individual or character associated with a genotype is called ....
10. The value of a character as determined by the genotype (genotypic value) and environmental interaction refers to ....
11. The additive genetic effects of an individual are passed on to its ....
12. Additive genetic effect is also referred to as ....
13. Non-additive effects and environmental effects cannot be passed to the ....
14. .... effects are not used for calculation of breeding value.
15. Variation in breeding value is ascribed to the .... effects of genes.

E. MARK TRUE OR FALSE

1. Breeding value is the property of the individual and the population from which its mates (parents) are selected.
2. The estimates of breeding value are specific to the genetic material and environment in which the material has been tested.
3. The estimates of breeding value vary according to the method of calculation.
4. Breeding values are estimated from phenotypic observations recorded on different traits of an individual.
5. Genotypic value is defined as the value of an individual or trait associated with a genotype.
6. A genetically superior individual is not necessarily a genetically superior parent.
7. Genetic value it refers to the value of genes to the individual itself.
8. The breeding value of an individual is influenced by several factors.
9. A parent passes on its genes but not its genotype to its progeny.
10. Breeding values are also used in the choice of breeding procedures for genetic improvement of various polygenic traits.
11. Breeding values of parents are useful in predicting the performance of their offspring.
12. Breeding values are also useful in making decisions for the selection of advanced generation breeding population.
13. In tree breeding, (forest breeding), breeding values are useful in the selection of superior stocks of timber trees.
14. In animal breeding, breeding values are used for selection of superior sire and dam for beef and milk production.
15. The mean value of the progeny of a parent is used to determine its genetic superiority as a parent.
16. Theoretical breeding value is calculated as sum of average effects of alleles of an individual.

F. USE APPROPRIATE TERM

1. The genetic worth of an individual that is transmitted to its offspring.
2. The value of an individual or character associated with a genotype.
3. The value of a character as determined by the genotype (genotypic value) and environmental interaction.
4. Measurement of the breeding value from the mean of its progeny.
5. The sum of average effects of genes over all loci or sum of average effects of alleles of an individual.

ANSWERS

MULTIPLE CHOICE

1. (d) All of these
2. (b) Animal breeding
3. (d) All of these
4. (d) All of these
5. (d) All of these
6. (d) All of these
7. (c) Both (a) and (b)
8. (d) All of these
9. (a) Additive variation
10. (d) All of these
11. (d) All of these
12. (d) All of these
13. (d) All of these
14. (a) Additive variance

FILL IN THE BLANKS

1. Worth
2. Offspring
3. Offspring
4. Offspring
5. Quality
6. Trait
7. Practical breeding value
8. Theoretical breeding value
9. Genotypic value
10. Phenotypic value
11. Progeny
12. Breeding value
13. Progeny
14. Non-additive
15. Additive

TRUE OR FALSE

1. True	2. True	3. True
4. True	5. True	6. True
7. True	8. True	9. True
10. True	11. True	12. True
13. True	14. True	15. True
16. True.		

APPROPRIATE TERM

1. Breeding value
2. Genotypic value
3. Phenotypic value
4. Practical Breeding value
5. Theoretical Breeding value

●●●

17

CHAPTER

Heterosis and Inbreeding Depression

A. DEFINITIONS

Heterosis. The superiority of F_1 in one or more characters over its parents; also called hybrid vigour.

Luxuriance. Superiority of F_1 over its parents in vegetative growth, but not in yield and adaptation; also called pseudo-heterosis.

Dominance. Masking effect of one allele over the other on the same locus.

Dominance hypothesis. Heterosis due to superiority of dominant alleles over recessive alleles. Heterosis is directly proportional to the number of dominant genes contributed by each parent.

Overdominance. The superiority of heterozygote over both the homozygotes.

Overdominance hypothesis. Heterosis due to superiority of heterozygote (Aa) over both homozygotes (AA and aa).

Epistasis. Interaction between alleles of two or more different loci.

Mid-Parent heterosis. Heterosis over the mean value of both parents; also called mean heterosis or average heterosis.

Economic heterosis. Superiority of F_1 hybrid over the commercial (popular) variety of a region; also called useful heterosis or standard heterosis or commercial heterosis.

Heterobeltiosis. Superiority of F_1 over better parents in one or more characters.

Inbreeding. Mating between closely related individuals such as selfing and sib-mating.

Inbreeders. Self pollinated plants or plant species; also called autogamous species.

Inbreeding depression. Loss or decrease in vigour and fitness due to inbreeding.

Hybrid. The progeny of a cross between genetically dissimilar parents.

Hybrid variety. The F_1 hybrid which is released either by State Variety Release Committee (SVRC) or Central Variety Release Committee (CVRC) for commercial cultivation in a particular region. Hybrids are of two types *viz.* intraspecific hybrid and interspecific hybrid (see later).

Inbred. In cross pollinated species, a true breeding line obtained by continuous inbreeding.

Outbreeding. Mating between less closely related individuals. Allogamy or cross pollution in an example of outbreeding.

Outbreders. Cross pollinated species; also called allogomous species.

Intraspecific hybrid. A hybrid between two varieties or genotypes of the same species; also called inter varietal hybrid. Intraspecific hybrids are of three types, *viz.* single, three-way and double cross hybrids.

Single cross hybrid. The hybrid progeny from a cross between two inbreeds or pure lines or varieties, *viz.* A × B.

Three-way cross hybrid. Hybrid progeny between a single cross and an inbred, *viz.* (A × B) × C.

Double cross hybrid. The hybrid progeny between two single crosses, *viz.* (A × B) × (C × D).

Top cross. A cross between an inbred line and an open pollinated variety; also called inbred-variety cross.

Double top cross. A cross between a single cross and an open pollinated variety, *viz.* (A × B) × OP variety.

Multiple cross. A cross involving more than four inbred lines; also called composite cross.

Polycross. Open pollination of a group of selected genotypes in isolation from other compatible genotypes to promote random mating among selected genotypes.

Interspecific hybrid. A hybrid between two different species of the same genes; also called intrageneric hybrid.

B. BACKGROUND INFORMATION

1. The term heterosis was coined by Shull in 1914.
2. In current usage, heterosis and hybrid vigour are used as synonyms and interchangeable.
3. The heterosis is confined only to the F_1 generation of a cross between genetically dissimilar parents.
4. The heterosis has positive association with specific combining ability variance.
5. The magnitude of heterosis is affected by genetic diversity, genetic base and adaptability of parents.
6. Heterosis can be fixed by asexual reproduction, apomixis, balanced polymorphism and polyploidy.
7. Heterosis can be estimated over mid parent, better parent, best local variety and commercial hybrid.
8. There are three possible genetic causes of heterosis, *viz.* dominance, overdominance, and epistasis.

9. The dominance hypothesis of heterosis was first proposed by Davenport in 1908.
10. The dominance hypothesis of heterosis was supported by Bruce (1910) and Keeble and Pellew (1910).
11. The dominance of linked gene hypothesis was proposed by Jones in 1917.
12. Collins (1921) provided explanation for symmetrical and smooth curve of genes in F_2 when the heterosis is governed by dominant genes.
13. The overdominance hypothesis of heterosis was independently proposed by Shull (1908) and East (1908).
14. The overdominance hypothesis of heterosis was supported by East (1936) and Hull (1945).
15. The term overdominance was coined by Hull in 1945 working with maize crop.
16. According to dominance hypothesis, heterosis results due to masking effects of dominant desirable alleles over harmful recessive alleles.
17. According to overdominance hypothesis, heterosis results due to complementation between divergent alleles received from two parents.
18. The epistasis, particularly which involves dominance effects (dominance × dominance) may contribute to heterosis.
19. The term useful heterosis was coined by Meredith and Bridge (1972) working with cotton crop.
20. Useful heterosis is also referred to as economic heterosis and has direct practical implications in plant breeding.
21. Overdominance hypothesis is also called as super dominance, single gene heterosis, stimulation of heterozygosis, comulative action of divergent alleles.
22. The formula $\frac{F_1 - MP}{MP} \times 100$ is used for estimation of mid-parent heterosis, where MP is the mean value of parents.
23. The heterobeltiosis is estimated as $\frac{F_1 - BP}{BP} \times 100$, where BP is the mean value of better parent.
24. The useful heterosis is calculated as $\frac{F_1 - CC}{CC} \times 100$, where CC is the mean value of commercial cultivar.
25. The inbreeding depression is calculated as $\frac{F_1 - F_2}{F_1} \times 100$.
26. The inbreeding depression results due to fixation of unfavourable recessive genes in F_2 generation.
27. Inbreeding of cross pollinated species leads to increase in homozygosity, genetic correlation between close relatives and genetic variability.
28. Outbreeding leads to reduction in homozygosity, genetic correlation between relatives and variability.

29. It high heterosis is followed by inbreeding depression, it indicates the presence of non-additive gene action (dominance and epistasis).

30. If the performance is almost same in F_1 and F_2, it reveals the presence of additive genes.

31. If the heterosis is negative in F_1 and there is increase in F_2, it again indicates presence of additive genes.

32. Negative heterosis is important for some characters such as earliness, micronaire value in cotton, plant height in cereals and low toxic substances like neurotoxin in *Lathyrus sativus*.

33. Inbreeders are homozygous and have advantage of homozygosity. They are tolerant to inbreeding.

34. Inbreeders have close (narrow) adaptation and are less flexible.

35. Outbreeders are heterozygous and have advantage of heterozygosity. They are intolerant to inbreeding.

36. Outbreeders have wide adaptation (adaptability) and are highly flexible.

37. Inbreeders do not permit new gene combinations.

38. Outbreeders permit new gene combinations.

39. Inbreeding is useful for maintaining the purity of characters.

40. Outbreeding is useful for combining desirablo genes from different sources into a single genotype.

41. Heterosis leads to increase in yield, reproductive ability, adaptability, general vigour, quality, etc.

42. Inbreeding depression leads to reduction in vigour, adaptation and reproductive ability.

43. The top cross method for evaluation of inbreds was first suggested by Davis in 1927.

44. The term luxuriance was coined by Renner in 1929.

45. Luxuriance is also called pseudo-heterosis.

C. MULTIPLE CHOICE

1. The term Heterosis was coined in 1914 by :

(a) Shull (b) East
(c) Hull (d) Davenport.

2. The term Heterosis was first used by Shull in :

(a) 1908 (b) 1910
(c) 1914 (d) 1945.

3. The dominance hypothesis of heterosis was first proposed in 1908 by :

(a) East (b) Shull
(c) Davenport (d) Hull.

4. Davenport proposed dominance hypothesis of heterosis in :

(a) 1908 (b) 1914
(c) 1945 (d) 1960.

5. Heterosis results due to :
(a) Dominance (b) Overdominance
(c) Epistasis (d) All of these.

6. Dominance hypothesis of heterosis was supported in 1910 by :
(a) Bruce (b) Keeble and Pellew
(c) (a) and (b) above (d) None of these.

7. The dominance of linked gene hypothesis was proposed in 1917 by :
(a) Daverport (b) Jones
(c) Collins (d) Shull.

8. Overdominance hypothesis of heterosis was proposed in 1908 by :
(a) Shull (b) East
(c) Bruce (d) East and Shull.

9. The term overdominance was coined in 1945 by :
(a) Shull (b) Hull
(c) Jones (d) East.

10. Hull coined the term overdominance in :
(a) 1908 (b) 1910
(c) 1945 (d) 1950.

11. Hull coined the term overdominance in 1945 working with :
(a) Wheat (b) Maize
(c) Garden pea (d) Cotton.

12. Which of the following types of epistasis contributes to heterosis ?
(a) Additive × additive (b) Additive × dominance
(c) Dominance × dominance (d) All of these.

13. The term useful heterosis was coined in 1972 by :
(a) Shull and East (b) Meredith and Bridge
(c) Mather and Jinks (d) None of these.

14. Meredith and Bridge coined the term useful heterosis in :
(a) 1945 (b) 1954
(c) 1966 (d) 1972.

15. Meredith and Bridge coined the term useful heterosis in 1972 working with
(a) Maize (b) Barley
(c) Cotton (d) Sorghum.

16. Overdominance heterosis is also called as :
(a) Super dominance (b) Single gene heterosis
(c) Stimulation of heterozygosis (d) All of these.

17. Heterosis is estimated over :
(a) Mid parent (b) Better parent
(c) Best local cultivar (d) All of these.

18. Which of the following properties of parents affect the magnitude of heterosis ?
(a) Genetic diversity (b) Genetic base
(c) Adaptability (d) All of these.

19. Heterosis can be fixed by :
(a) Asexual reproduction (b) Apromixis
(c) Polyploidy (d) All of these.

20. Heterosis over the best commercial cultivar of a locality is called :
(a) Mid parent heterosis (b) Heterobeltiosis
(c) Useful heterosis (d) All of these.

21. Which of the following terms was coined by Meredith and Bridge in 1972 ?
(a) Mean heterosis (b) Heterobeltiosis
(c) Useful heterosis (d) None of these.

22. Heterobeltiosis is estimated over :
(a) Mid-parent (b) Better parent
(c) Popular variety (d) Popular hybrid.

23. Useful heterosis is estimated over :
(a) Mid parent (b) Popular variety
(c) Better parent (d) Best parent.

24. The formula $\frac{F_1 - BP}{BP} \times 100$ is used for calculation of :
(a) Heterobeltiosis (b) Mean heterosis
(c) Useful heterosis (d) Pseudo heterosis.

25. The formula $\frac{F_1 - F_2}{F_1} \times 100$ is used for estimation of :
(a) Useful heterosis (b) Heterobeltiosis
(c) Average heterosis (d) Inbreeding depression.

26. Which of the following formula is used for estimation of useful heterosis ?
(a) $\frac{F_1 - MP}{MP} \times 100$ (b) $\frac{F_1 - BP}{BP} \times 100$
(c) $\frac{F_1 - CC}{CC} \times 100$ (d) $\frac{F_1 - F_2}{F_1} \times 100$.

27. Inbreeding of cross pollinated species tends to increase in :
(a) Homozygosity (b) Genetic correlation
(c) Genetic diversity (d) All of these.

28. Outbreeding tends to reduction in :
(a) Homozygosity (b) Genetic correlation
(c) Genetic variability (d) All of these.

29. Negative heterosis is important for :
(a) Earliness (b) Plant height in cereals
(c) Low toxic substances (d) All of these.

30. Heterosis leads to increase in :
(a) Yield (b) General vigour
(c) Adaptation (d) All of these.

31. Inbreeding leads to reduction in :
(a) General vigour (b) Adaptation
(c) Reproductive ability (d) All of these.

32. A cross between two inbreds is called :
(a) Single cross (b) Three way cross
(c) Double cross (d) Multiple cross.

33. Highest uniformity is observed in a :
(a) Single cross (b) Three-way cross
(c) Double cross (d) Multiple cross.

34. An inbred-variety cross is known as :
(a) Three-way cross (b) Double cross
(c) Top Cross (d) Polycross.

35. Mating between a single cross and an open pollinated variety is called :
(a) Polycross (b) Composite cross
(c) Top cross (d) Double top cross.

36. Heterosis can be fully exploited in the form of :
(a) Hybrids (b) Composites
(c) Synthetics (d) Multilines.

37. Top cross method for evaluation of inbreds was first suggested in 1927 by :
(a) Richey (b) Davis
(c) Jenkins (d) Jones.

38. The cross pollinated species are also called as :
(a) Outbreeders (b) Allogamous species
(c) (a) and (b) above (d) Autogamous species.

39. Self pollinated species are also termed as :
(a) Autogamous species (b) Inbreeders
(c) (a) and (b) above (d) Allogamous species.

40. Inbreeders have :
(a) Selfing (b) Homozygosity
(c) Close adaptation (d) All of these.

41. Outbreeders have ?
(a) Random mating (b) Heterozygosity
(c) Wide adaptation (d) All of these.

D. FILL IN THE BLANKS

1. Superiority of F_1 in fitness and vigour over its parents is called ....

2. The term heterosis was coined by ....

3. The term heterosis was first used by Shull in ....

4. Heterosis is also called ....

5. The superiority of F_1 over its parents in vegetative growth is known as ....

6. The term Luxuriance was coined by ....
7. Renner coined the term Luxuriance in the year ....
8. Luxuriance is also called ....
9. .... proposed dominance hypothesis of heterosis in 1908.
10. The dominance of linked gene hypothesis was proposed by ....
11. .... and .... proposed overdominance hypothesis of heterosis in 1908.
12. The term overdominance was coined by ....
13. Hull first used the term overdominance in ....
14. Hull developed the concept of overdominance working with ....
15. The term useful heterosis was coined by ....
16. Meredith and Bridge coined the term useful heterosis in ....
17. The concept of useful heterosis was developed by Meredith and Bridge working with ....
18. Useful heterosis is also called ....
19. Heterosis over the mean value of both the parents is called ....
20. Heterosis over the better parent is called ....
21. Heterosis over the best commercial variety is known as ....
22. The superiority of heterozygote over both the homozygotes is termed ....
23. Intra-allelic interaction refers to ....
24. Interallelic interaction refers to ....
25. Mating between closely related individuals is called ....
26. Mating between distantly related individuals is known as ....
27. Loss in vigour and fitness due to inbreeding is termed ....
28. The progeny of a cross between genetically dissimilar parents is called ....
29. F_1 hybrid which is grown for commercial cultivation is called ....
30. .... refers to self pollinated species.
31. .... refers to cross pollinated species.
32. An intervarietal cross is also called ....
33. An interspecific cross is also known as ....
34. .... refers to a cross between two inbreds or pure lines.
35. .... refers to the progeny between a single cross and an inbred.
36. The progeny obtained by crossing between two single crosses is called ....
37. Inbred-variety cross refers to ....
38. Multiple cross is also called ....
39. Super dominance refers to ....
40. A cross between a single cross and an open pollinated variety is called ....

E. MARK TRUE OR FALSE

1. The term heterosis was coined in 1914 by East.
2. Heterosis is also called hybrid vigour.
3. The term Luxuriance was first used by Jones.
4. Luxuriance is also called useful heterosis.
5. Dominance refers to intra-allelic interaction.
6. Epistasis refers to interallelic interaction.
7. The dominance hypothesis of heterosis was proposed by East.
8. Jones proposed dominance of linked gene hypothesis.
9. The term overdominance was coined by Shull.
10. The overdominance hypothesis was coined by Shull.
11. Meredith and Bridge coined the term useful heterosis.
12. Useful heterosis is also called economic heterosis.
13. Heterobeltiosis refers to heterosis over mid parent.
14. Mean heterosis refers to heterosis over better parent.
15. Inbreeding refers to mating between closely related individuals.
16. Mating between distantly related individuals is called outbreeding.
17. Self pollination is an example of inbreeding.
18. Cross pollination is an example of outbreeding.
19. Intervarietal cross is also called interspecific cross.
20. Intergeneric cross involves two species of the same genes.
21. A single cross involves two inbred lines.
22. A double cross involves four inbred lines.
23. A three-way cross involves two inbred lines.
24. A multiple cross is also called composite cross.
25. A multiple cross involves more than four inbred lines.
26. The maximum uniformity is found in double cross progeny
27. Top cross refers to an inbred variety cross.
28. The top cross is common in wheat.
29. Self pollinated species are called inbreeders.
30. Cross pollinated species are called outbreeders.
31. Inbreeders have wide adaptation.
32. Outbreders have close adaptation.
33. Inbreds are obtained by sib-mating.
34. Pure lines are obtained by selfing.
35. Heterosis can be fully exploited in the form of synthetics.
36. Inbreeding leads to loss in vigour and fitness.
37. Heterosis leads to increase in vigour and fitness.

38. Luxuriance leads to increase in fitness.
39. Overdominance in also called superdominance.
40. Negative heterosis is desirable for toxic substances.

F. USE APPROPRIATE TERM

1. Superiority of F_1 in one or more characters over its parents.
2. Superiority of F_1 over its parents in vegetative growth.
3. Intra-allelic gene interaction.
4. Interallelic gene interaction.
5. Heterosis due to superiority of heterozygote over homozygotes.
6. Superiority of F_1 over mean value of both the parents.
7. Superiority of F_1 over the better parent.
8. Superiority of F_1 over the commercial variety of a region.
9. Mating between closely related individuals.
10. Mating between distantly related individuals.
11. The progeny of a cross between genetically dissimilar parents.
12. A true breeding line obtained by continuous inbreeding.
13. A cross between two genotypes of the same species.
14. A cross between two species of the same genus.
15. A cross involving two inbreds or pure lines.
16. A cross involving three inbred lines or pure lines.
17. A cross involving four inbred lines.
18. A cross involving more than four inbred lines.
19. A cross between an inbred line and open pollinated variety.
20. A cross between a single cross and an open pollinated variety.
21. Open pollination of a group of selected genotypes in isolation from other compatible genotypes to promote random mating among selected genotypes.
22. A hybrid cultivated on commercial scale.

ANSWERS

MULTIPLE CHOICE

1. (a) Shull
2. (c) 1914
3. (c) Davenport
4. (a) 1908
5. (d) All of these
6. (c) (a) and (b)
7. (b) Jones
8. (d) East and Shull
9. (b) Hull
10. (c) 1945
11. (b) Maize
12. (c) Dominance × dominance
13. (b) Meredith and Bridge
14. (d) 1972
15. (c) Cotton
16. (d) All of these
17. (d) All of these

18. (d) All of these
19. (d) All of these
20. (c) Useful heterosis
21. (c) Useful heterosis
22. (b) Better parent
23. (b) Popular variety
24. (a) Heterobeltiosis
25. (d) Inbreeding depression
26. (c) $\frac{F_1 - CC}{CC} \times 100$
27. (d) All of these
28. (d) All of these
29. (d) All of these
30. (d) All of these
31. (d) All of these
32. (a) Single cross
33. (a) Single cross
34. (c) Top cross
35. (d) Double top cross
36. (a) Hybrids
37. (b) Davis
38. (c) (a) and (b)
39. (c) (a) and (b)
40. (d) All of these
41. (d) All of these

FILL IN THE BLANKS

1. Heterosis
2. Shull
3. 1914
4. Hybrid vigour
5. Luxuriance
6. Renner
7. 1929
8. Pseudo heterosis
9. Davenport
10. Jones
11. East, Shull
12. Hull
13. 1945
14. Maize
15. Meredith and Bridge
16. 1972
17. Cotton
18. Economic heterosis
19. Mid-parent heterosis
20. Heterobeltiosis
21. Economic/Useful heterosis
22. Overdominance
23. Dominance
24. Epistasis
25. Inbreeding
26. Outbreeding
27. Inbreeding depression
28. Hybrid
29. Hybrid variety
30. Inbreeders
31. Outbreeders
32. Intraspecific cross
33. Intrageneric cross
34. Single cross
35. Three-way cross
36. Double cross
37. Top cross
38. Composite cross
39. Overdominance
40. Double top cross.

TRUE OR FALSE

1. False **2.** True **3.** False
4. False **5.** True **6.** True
7. False **8.** True **9.** False
10. False **11.** True **12.** True
13. False **14.** False **15.** True
16. True **17.** True **18.** True
19. False **20.** False **21.** True
22. True **23.** False **24.** True
25. True **26.** False **27.** True
28. False **29.** True **30.** True
31. False **32.** False **33.** True
34. True **35.** False **36.** True
37. True **38.** False **39.** True
40. True

APPROPRIATE TERM

1. Heterosis
2. Luxuriance
3. Dominance
4. Epistasis
5. Overdominance
6. Average/Mean heterosis
7. Heterobeltiosis
8. Useful/Economic heterosis
9. Inbreeding
10. Outbreeding
11. Hybrid
12. Inbred
13. Intervarietal or Intraspecific cross
14. Interspecific cross
15. Single cross
16. Three-way cross
17. Double cross
18. Multiple/Composite cross
19. Top cross
20. Double top cross
21. Polycross
22. Hybrid variety

18

CHAPTER

Introductory Statistics

A. DEFINITIONS

Arithmetic mean. Sum of all observations in a sample divided by their number.

Dispersion. The degree to which numerical data tend to spread about the mean value. It is a measure of variation in a sample.

Range. Difference between the lowest and the highest values present in the observations in a sample.

Standard deviation. The square root of the squares of the deviations measured from the mean. It is the square root of variance.

Variance. The average of the squared deviations from the mean or the square of the standard deviation.

Coefficient of variation. The percentage ratio of standard deviation of a sample to its mean.

Standard error. The measure of the mean difference between sample mean and population parameter. It is a measure of uncontrolled variation present in a sample.

Null hypothesis. A hypothesis of no difference between sample mean and population parameter.

Tests of significance. Various statistical procedures which are used to decide whether the differences under study are significant or non-significant.

Tests of significance include χ^2-test, t-test, z-test and F-test.

χ^2-test. A test of statistical significance which is used to test the significance of differences between observed and expected frequencies. It is used for the analysis of oligogenic characters.

Degree of freedom. The number of independent comparisons.

t-test. A test of significance which is used for comparing two means when sample size is small (upto 30). It is of two types : Student t-used when observations are paired, and Fisher's t-used when observations are unpaired.

***z*-test.** A test of significance which is used to compare two means when the sample size is large (more than 30).

B. BACKGROUND INFORMATION

1. Statistics is a branch of applied mathematics which deals with the collection, presentation, analysis and interpretation of numerical data.
2. There are three types of statistics, *viz.* first degree, second degree and third degree.
3. First degree statistics includes mean. It is used for analysis of generation means, heterosis, combining ability effects, metroglyph analysis, stability analysis etc.
4. First degree statistics is also called first order statistics.
5. Second degree statistics includes estimates of variances and covariances. It is used for estimation of correlations, path, discriminant function, genetic advance, combining ability variances, heritability, components of genetic variance etc.
6. Second degree statistics is also known as second order statistics.
7. Third degree statistics includes skewness and curtosis which are used in fitting frequency curves, surfaces and flatness.
8. Third degree statistics is also termed high order statistics.
9. Mean is used for measurement of all types of parameters.
10. The calculation of mean is based on all observations of a sample.
11. Mean is very much affected by values of extreme observations in a sample.
12. Range is a measure of the spread of variation in a sample.
13. Standard deviation is the square root of a variance.
14. Standard error is the measure of uncontrolled (environmental) variation present in a sample.
15. Standard error is calculated as $\frac{SD}{\sqrt{N}}$.
16. The coefficient of variation is calculated as $\frac{SD}{\overline{X}} \times 100$.
17. The measure of the coefficient of variation was evolved by Karl Pearson.
18. The coefficient of variation does not have any unit.
19. The Null hypothesis was given by R.A. Fisher.
20. The χ^2 test was developed by Karl Pearson.
21. In plant breeding, χ^2 test is used for the study of segregation ratio, linkage and gene frequencies.
22. The general formula of χ^2 test is $\Sigma\ (O - E)^2/E$.
23. The statistical procedures which are used to decide whether the differences under study are significant or non-significant are called tests of significance.
24. The commonly used tests of significance include *z*-test, *t*-test and F-test.

25. z-test is used when the sample size is large (more than 30).
26. t-test is used when the sample size is small (less than 30). It is of two types *viz.* Student t and Fisher t.
27. Student t is used when observations are paired.
28. Fisher t is used when observations are not paired.
29. The F-test is used to test the significance of difference among several means.
30. z-test and t-test are used to test the significance of difference between two means.
31. The measure of regression coefficient was evolved by Sir Francis Galton.
32. The value of regression and correlation coefficients is the same when the correlation between two variables is perfect.
33. Regression is expressed in the unit of measurement of variable.
34. Correlation is independent of the unit of measurement.
35. In augmented design check varieties are replicated and germplasm lines are non-replicated.
36. Augmented design is used for evaluation of large number of germplasm lines.

C. MULTIPLE CHOICE

1. Statistics deals with which aspect of numerical data :
   (a) Collection (b) Analysis
   (c) Interpretation (d) All of these.
2. The degree of statistics is of :
   (a) First order (b) Second order
   (c) Third order (d) All of these.
3. First degree statistics deals with :
   (a) Means (b) Variances
   (c) Covariances (d) All of these.
4. Second degree statistics deals with :
   (a) Variances (b) Covariances
   (c) Variances and covariances (d) Means.
5. Third degree statistics deals with :
   (a) Skewness (b) Curtosis
   (c) Means (d) (a) and (b).
6. High order statistics refers to :
   (a) First order statistics (b) Second order statistics
   (c) Third order statistics (d) None of these.
7. Measure of uncontrolled variation refers to :
   (a) Standard error (b) Standard deviation
   (c) Mean (d) Range.
8. The difference between lowest and highest values in a sample refers to :
   (a) Range (b) Mean
   (c) Standard error (d) Standard deviation.

9. The square root of the variance refers to :
(a) Standard deviation (b) Mean deviation
(c) Standard error (d) None of these.

10. The coefficient of variation was evolved by :
(a) Fisher (b) Karl Pearson
(c) Galton (d) Yates.

11. Standard deviation is the square root of :
(a) Range (b) Variance
(c) Standard error (d) None of these.

12. Null hypothesis was given by :
(a) Galton (b) Fisher
(c) Karl Pearson (d) Smith.

13. The χ^2 test was developed by :
(a) Karl Pearson (b) Galton
(c) Fisher (d) Yates.

14. χ^2 test is used for the study of :
(a) Segregation ratio (b) Linkage
(c) Gene frequencies (d) All of these.

15. Tests of significance include :
(a) *z*-test (b) *t*-test
(c) F-test (d) All of these.

16. The value of regression and correlation is the same when the correlation between two variables is :
(a) Positive (b) Negative
(c) Perfect (d) Imperfect.

17. The formula $\frac{SD}{\sqrt{N}}$ is used for the estimation of :
(a) Range (b) Variance
(c) Standard error (d) Standard deviation.

18. The formula $\frac{SD}{\overline{X}} \times 100$ is used for calculation of :
(a) Arithmetic mean (b) Coefficient of variation
(c) Standard error (d) None of these.

19. The formula $\frac{\Sigma X}{N}$ is used for the estimation of :
(a) Arithmetic mean (b) Range
(c) Standard error (d) Coefficient of variation.

20. The formula $\Sigma (O - E)^2/E$ is used in :
(a) F-test (b) *z*-test
(c) χ^2-test (d) *t*-test.

21. Segregation ratio can be tested with the help of :
    (a) t-test (b) z-test
    (c) χ^2-test (d) F-test.

D. FILL IN THE BLANKS

1. Statistics is a branch of ....
2. The first degree statistics is called ....
3. The second degree statistics is known as ....
4. The third degree statistics is termed as ....
5. The first degree statistics includes ....
6. The second degree statistics includes ....
7. The third degree statistics includes ....
8. The spread of variation in a sample can be known through ....
9. Square root of variance is called ....
10. Standard error is calculated as ....
11. The coefficient of variation is calculated as ....
12. The coefficient of variation was evolved by ....
13. The Null hypothesis was given by ....
14. ....developed the χ^2-test.
15. The general formula of χ^2-test is ....
16. The goodness of fit of a segregation ratio is tested with the help of ....
17. z-test is used when the sample size is ....
18. t-test is used when the sample size is ....
19. Student's t is used when observations are ....
20. Fisher's t is used when observations are ....
21. The measure of regression coefficient was evolved by ....

E. MARK TRUE OR FALSE

1. Statistics is a branch of basic mathematics.
2. The first degree statistics is also called high order statistics.
3. The second degree statistics includes skewness and curtosis.
4. Standard deviation is the square root of variance.
5. Standard error is calculated as $\frac{SD}{\sqrt{N}}$
6. The coefficient of variation was evolved by Fisher.
7. The coefficient of variation is estimated as $\frac{SD}{\sqrt{N}} \times 100$.
8. The coefficient of variation does not have any unit.

9. The Null hypothesis was given by Yates.
10. The χ^2-test was evolved by Karl Pearson.
11. The χ^2-test is also called the test of goodness of fit.
12. z-test is used when sample size is small.
13. t-test is used when sample size is large.
14. Student's t is used when observations are paired.
15. Fisher's t is used when observations are not paired.
16. The regression analysis was evolved by Pearson.
17. Regression is measured in the unit of measurement of variable.
18. Correlation is independent of the unit of measurement.

F. USE APPROPRIATE TERM

1. A scientifically planned method.
2. The number of independent comparison.
3. The difference between the highest and the lowest value in the observations of a sample.
4. The square root of the variance.
5. The measure of uncontrolled variance.
6. The square of the standard deviation.
7. The hypothesis of no difference between sample mean and population mean.
8. A test of significance for comparing several means.
9. A test used for testing the goodness of fit of segregation ratios.
10. A test used for comparing small sample of two means.
11. A test used for comparing large sample of two means.

ANSWERS

MULTIPLE CHOICE

1. (d) All of these
2. (d) All of these
3. (a) Mean
4. (c) Variances and Covariances
5. (d) (a) and (b)
6. (c) Third order statistics
7. (a) Standard error
8. (a) Range
9. (a) Standard deviation
10. (b) Karl Pearson
11. (b) Variance
12. (b) Fisher
13. (a) Karl Pearson
14. (d) All of these
15. (d) All of these
16. (c) Perfect
17. (c) Standard error
18. (b) Coefficient of variation
19. (a) Arithmetic mean
20. (c) χ^2-test
21. (c) χ^2-test

FILL IN THE BLANKS

1. Applied Mathematics
2. First order statistics
3. Second order statistics
4. Third order statistics
5. Mean
6. Variances and covariances
7. Skewness and Curtosis
8. Range
9. Standard deviation
10. $\frac{SD}{\sqrt{N}}$
11. $\frac{SD}{\overline{X}} \times 100$
12. Karl Pearson
13. R.A. Fisher
14. Karl Pearson
15. $\Sigma (O - E)^2/E$
16. χ^2-test
17. Large
18. Small
19. Paired
20. Unpaired
21. Galton

TRUE OR FALSE

1. False	2. False	3. False
4. True	5. True	6. False
7. True	8. True	9. False
10. True	11. True	12. False
13. False	14. True	15. True
16. False	17. True	18. True

APPROPRIATE TERM

1. Experiment
2. Degree of Freedom
3. Range
4. Standard Deviation
5. Standard error
6. Variance
7. Null Hypothesis
8. F-test
9. χ^2-test
10. t-test
11. z-test

●●●

19

CHAPTER

Experimental Designs

A. DEFINITIONS

Analysis of variance. The statistical procedure which separates the total variation into different physical components.

Analysis of covariance. The statistical procedure which splits simultaneously the variation of two variables in various components.

Regression coefficient. A measure of change in the dependent variable with unit change in independent variable. The value of regression and correlation is the same when there is perfect correlation between two variables.

Experimental design. Various types of plot arrangements which are used to test a set of treatments to draw valid conclusion about a particular problem.

Experimental error. Variation due to environmental factors or uncontrolled factors.

Experimental unit. The group of material to which a treatment is applied in a single trial or experiment. It may be a plot of land, a group of cattle in dairy and a patient in a hospital.

Replication. Repetition of treatments under investigation.

Randomization. The process of random allocation of treatments to different plots in an experiment.

Local control. The principle of making use of greater homogeneity in groups of experimental units for reducing experimental error. Also called error control.

F-test. A test of statistical significance which is used to compare the differences among several means.

F-value. The ratio of treatment variance to the error variance.

Correction factor. The square of grand total divided by number observations in the analysis of variance.

Critical difference. Least significant difference, greater than which all the differences are significant.

Completely randomized design. Experimental design which is used when the experimental plot is small and homogeneous such as pot culture.

Randomized block design. Experimental design which controls fertility variation in one direction only.

Latin square design. Experimental design which simultaneously controls fertility variation in two directions.

Split plot design. Experimental design in which experimental plots are divided into main plots, subplots and ultimate plots. In this design several factors are studied simultaneously with different levels of precision.

Lattice design. Incomplete block design in which the number of varieties or treatments forms a square.

Augmented design. An experimental design which is used to test a large number of germplasm lines in a limited area.

B. BACKGROUND INFORMATION

1. The procedure of analysis of variance was evolved by R.A. Fisher.
2. Principles of experimental designs include replications, randomization and local control.
3. Local control is also known as error control.
4. Increase in replication increases the precision by reducing the experimental error.
5. Randomization gives equal chance to all treatments for being allotted to plots with high and low fertility level.
6. Randomization reduces variations caused by scattered fertility in the field.
7. Completely Randomized Design (CRD) is useful for pot culture experiments.
8. Local control is not adopted in CRD.
9. Randomized Block Design (RBD) controls fertility variation in one direction only.
10. Latin Square Design (LSD) controls fertility variation in two directions.
11. In LSD, the number of replications per treatment is always equal to the number of treatments.
12. Split Plot Design (SPD) consists of main plots, sub plots and ultimate plots.
13. Lattice design is used when number of treatments is sufficiently large and forms square.
14. Lattice designs are also called incomplete block designs.
15. The concept of augmented design was developed by Federer in 1956.
16. In augmented design check varieties are replicated and germplasm lines are non-replicated.
17. Augmented design is used for evaluation of large number of germplasm lines.

C. MULTIPLE CHOICE

1. The procedure of analysis of variance was evolved by :
   (a) Galton (b) Fisher
   (c) Yates (d) Karl Pearson.

2. In which design, the number of treatments and replications is the same ?
(a) CRD (b) RBD
(c) LSD (d) None of these.

3. In which design, the number of treatment should form square ?
(a) Latin square design (b) Augmented design.
(c) Lattice design (d) RBD

4. Local control is not adopted in :
(a) RBD (b) CRD
(c) LSD (d) Lattice design.

5. Which design is suitable for evaluating several hundred lines of germplasm ?
(a) Lattice design (b) Randomized Block Design
(c) Augmented design (d) CRD.

6. Which of the following designs consists of main plots, subplots and ultimate plots ?
(a) CRD (b) Lattice design
(c) Split plot design (d) Augmented design.

7. Incomplete designs refer to :
(a) RBD (b) Latin square design
(c) Lattice Designs (d) Augmented Design.

8. The concept of augmented design was developed by :
(a) Galton (b) Fisher
(c) Federer (d) Pearson.

9. Augmented design is used for evaluation of :
(a) Advanced cultures (b) Segregating material
(c) Germplasm (d) Hybrids.

10. Federer developed the concept of augmented design in :
(a) 1946 (b) 1956
(c) 1966 (d) 1970.

11. Analysis of variance permits estimation of :
(a) Phenotypic variance (b) Genotypic variance
(c) Environmental variance (d) All of these.

12. The ratio of treatment variance to error variance is called :
(a) Critical difference (b) Correction factor
(c) F-value (d) *t*-value.

13. Local control is also called :
(a) Standard error (b) Experimental error
(c) Error control (d) None of these.

14. Latin square design can efficiently evaluate upto :
(a) 8 treatments (b) 12 treatments
(c) 15 treatments (d) All of these.

15. RBD can efficiently evaluate upto :
(a) 20 treatments (b) 30 treatments
(c) 35 treatments (d) 40 treatments.

D. FILL IN THE BLANKS

1. The analysis of variance was evolved by ....
2. Local control is also known as ....
3. Local control is not adopted in ....
4. .... design is used when number of treatments is large and form square.
5. Lattice design is also called .... design.
6. The design in which number of treatments and replications is the same refers to ....
7. The ratio of treatment variance to error variance is called ....
8. Variance ratio is also called ....
9. Repetition of treatments under investigation refers to ....
10. A scientifically planned method is called ....
11. The number of independent comparisons refers to ....
12. The concept of augmented design was developed by ....
13. Federer developed the concept of augmented design in ....
14. The value of regression and correlation is the same when the comparison between two variables is ....
15. The objects of comparison are called ....
16. The hypothesis of no difference between sample mean and population parameter is called ....
17. .... controls fertility variation in one direction only.
18. .... controls fertility variation in two directions.
19. .... is used when the experimental material is limited and plots are homogeneous.

E. MARK TRUE OR FALSE

1. The analysis of variance was evolved by Yates.
2. Local control is also called error control.
3. Lattice design is also known as incomplete block design.
4. In Latin square design, the number of treatments and replications is the same.
5. The concept of augmented design was developed by Fisher.
6. The variance ratio is also called F-value.
7. Experiment refers to a scientifically planned method.
8. Increase in replication increases the precision.
9. Increase in replication reduces the experimental error.
10. Latin Square Design controls fertility variation in one direction only.
11. In Lattice design, number of treatments should form square.
12. CRD is used for pot culture experiments.

F. USE APPROPRIATE TERM

1. An experimental design in which the number of treatments and replications is the same.
2. An experimental design in which the number of treatments form square.

3. Repetition of treatments under investigation.
4. The process of random allocation of treatments to different plots in an experiment.
5. An experimental design which is used to test large number of germplasm lines in limited area.
6. The ratio of treatment variance to error variance.
7. Various objects of comparison in an experiment.
8. A measure of change in the dependent variable with unit change in independent variable.
9. The ratio of standard deviation to its mean.

ANSWERS

MULTIPLE CHOICE

1. (b) Fisher
2. (c) LSD
3. (c) Lattice design
4. (b) CRD
5. (c) Augmented design
6. (c) Split plot design
7. (c) Lattice design
8. (c) Federer
9. (c) Germplasm
10. (b) 1956
11. (d) All of these
12. (c) F-value
13. (c) Error control
14. (a) 8 treatments
15. (d) 20 treatments

FILL IN THE BLANKS

1. Fisher
2. Error control
3. CRD
4. Lattice
5. Incomplete block
6. Latin Square Design
7. F-value
8. F-value
9. Replecation
10. Experiment
11. Degree of freedom
12. Federer
13. 1956
14. Perfect
15. Treatments
16. Null hypothesis
17. RBD
18. LSD
19. CRD

TRUE OR FALSE

1. False	2. True	3. True
4. True	5. False	6. True
7. True	8. True	9. True
10. False	11. True	12. True

APPROPRIATE TERM

1. Latin Square Design
2. Lattice Design
3. Replication
4. Randomization
5. Augmented Design
6. F-value
7. Treatments
8. Regression coefficient
9. Coefficient of variation

●●●

20

CHAPTER

Introduction to Computers

A. DEFINITIONS

Computer. An electronic device that can transmit, store and process information or data. Computers are of four types, *viz.* micro computer, mini computer, main frame computer and super computer.

Micro computer. A computer that is designed using a microprocessor as its central processing unit (CPU). It includes four components : microprocessor, memory, input, and output.

Mini computer. A medium size computer which is more costly and powerful than micro computer.

Main frame computers. Computers with large storage capacity and very high speed of processing as compared to micro and mini computers.

Super computer. A computer with extremely large storage capacity and atleast 10 times faster computing speed than other computers. Such computers are used in scientific and engineering disciplines.

Bit. A binary digit, 0 and 1.

Byte. A group of 8 bits.

Bus. A group of lines used to transfer bits between microprocessor and the components of computer system.

Microprocessor. A semi conductor device manufactured by using large scale integration technique. It includes arithmetic logic unit (ALU), register arrays and control circuit on a single chip.

Floppy Disk. A thin plastic coated disk with magnetic oxide which is used for information storage in computers.

Hard Disk. A disk which is permanently fixed in a computer, also called Winchester disk. Hard disks have more storage capacity and are faster in reading and writing.

Nibble. A group of four bits.

Programme. A set of instructions written in a specific sequence for the computer to accomplish a given task.

Software. A group of programmes.

Hardware. The physical components of the computers such as key board, processing unit, monitor and printer.

Memory. A medium that stores binary information such as instructions and data, and provides that information to the microprocessor whenever necessary. Memory is of two types, *viz.*, read only memory and read and write memory.

Read only memory (ROM). A memory that stores binary information permanently. The information can be read from this memory but cannot be altered.

Read/write memory (R/WR). A memory that stores binary information during the operation of computer. This is used as writing pad to write user's program and data. The information stored in this memory can be read and altered easily.

Word. A group of bits the computer can recognise and process at a time.

B. BACKGROUND INFORMATION

1. Computers are electronic devices which can input, store and manipulate data and output information in a desired form.
2. Computers have some important features such as high speed, high accuracy, versatile nature, automation capacity, diligence and high storage capacity.
3. Computers are classified on the basis of operating principle, application and size, and capacity.
4. Based on operating principle, computers are of three types, *viz.* digital, analog and hybrid computers.
5. Digital computers operate by counting.
6. Analog computers operate by measuring.
7. Hybrid computers operate by both counting and measuring.
8. Based on applications, computers are of two types, *viz.*, general purpose and special porpose computers.
9. Based on size and capacity, computers are of four types, *viz.*, microcomputers, mini computers, main frame and super computers.
10. Micro computers are designed for use by one person at a time.
11. Micro computers are also called personal computers.
12. Mini computer is designed to serve multiple users at a time.
13. Main frame computers have large storage capacity and very high speed of processing and are meant for multiple users.
14. Super computers have extremely large storage capacity and also extremely high computing speed.
15. Computers are classified into four generations, *viz.*, first, second, third and fourth generation.

16. In first generation computers, vacuum tube is used as the main component.

17. In second generation computers, transistor is used as the main component.

18. In third generation computers, integrated circuits (IC chips) are used as main components.

19. In fourth generation computers, large scale Integrated circuits (LIC chips) are used as main components.

20. Air conditioning is not required for fourth generation computers.

21. First generation computers were developed during 1946-1955.

22. Second generation computers were developed during 1956-1965.

23. Third generation computers were developed during 1966-1995.

24. Fourth generation computers were developed since 1996 onwards.

25. A micro computer includes four components, *viz.,* micro processor, input, output and memory.

26. The micro processor is a semi-conductor device made of electronic logic circuits.

27. The micro processor consists of three units, *viz.* arithmetic logic unit (ALU), register unit and control unit.

28. The memory is of two types, *viz.* read only memory (ROM) and read/write memory.

29. In ROM, programs can be read, they can not be altered.

30. Read/write memory is also called random access memory (RAM) or user memory.

31. The information stored in RAM can be read and altered easily.

32. Input device includes key board.

33. Output devices include monitor and printer.

34. The input and output devices are known as peripherals.

35. The physical components of computer are called hardware.

36. Hardware includes keyboard, central processing unit, monitor and printer.

37. A set of instructions written for the computer to perform a task is called a program.

38. A group of programs is called software.

39. Floppy diskettes are used as external storage device.

40. Floppy disks are available in 8 inch, 5.25 inch and 3.5 inch sizes.

41. The hard disk is also known as Winchester disk.

42. Hard disks are available in four sizes, *viz.* 5.25 inch, 8 inch, 10.5 inch and 14 inch.

43. The smallest size computer is palmtop computer.

44. Laptop and palmtop are portable computers.

45. A group of 8 bits refers to byte.

C. MULTIPLE CHOICE

1. The smallest computer refers to :

(a) Desktop (b) Palmtop
(c) Laptop (d) None of these.

2. How many persons can work with micro computer ?
(a) One (b) Two
(c) Three (d) Several.

3. The size of mini computer is :
(a) Small (b) Medium
(c) Large (d) Very large.

4. The storage capacity of mainframe computers is :
(a) Small (b) Medium
(c) Large (d) Extremely large.

5. The computing speed of super computer is :
(a) Medium (b) High
(c) Very high (d) Extremely high.

6. In fourth generation computers, the main component is :
(a) Vacuum table (b) Transistor
(c) Integrated circuit (d) Large scale integrated circuits.

7. In first generation computers, internal storage device is :
(a) Electrostatic tubes (b) Magnetic core
(c) Semiconductor memory (d) All of these.

8. The speed of operation is very high in :
(a) Mini computers (b) Micro computers
(c) Main frames (d) Super computers.

9. Personal computer refers to :
(a) Mini computers (b) Micro computers
(c) Main frames (d) Super computer.

10. The first electronic computing machine was introduced in :
(a) 1930s (b) 1940s
(c) 1950s (d) 1960s.

11. The computers developed during 1946-1955 refer to :
(a) First generation (b) Second generation
(c) Third generation (d) Fourth generation.

12. The second generation computers were developed during :
(a) 1946-1965 (b) 1956-1965
(c) 1966-1975 (d) 1976-1985.

13. In which generation of computer floppy disk is used ?
(a) First generation (b) Second generation
(c) Third generation (d) Fourth generation.

14. In which generation of computer air conditioning is not required ?
(a) First generation (b) Second generation
(c) Third generation (d) Fourth generation.

15. In which generation of computer Large Scale Integrated circuits are used as main components ?
(a) Third generation (b) Second generation
(c) Fourth generation (d) All of these.

16. The computers have high :
(a) Speed (b) Accuracy
(c) Storage capacity (d) All of these.

17. How many times super computers are faster than other computers ?
(a) Four times (b) 5 times
(c) 10 times (d) 20 times.

18. Computers are classified on the basis of :
(a) Operating principle (b) Size and capacity
(c) Applications (d) All of these.

19. Digital computers operate by :
(a) Counting (b) Measuring
(c) Counting and measuring (d) Processing.

20. Analog computers operate by :
(a) Measuring (b) Counting
(c) Processing (d) (a) and (b).

21. Hybrid computers operate by :
(a) Counting and measuring (b) Measuring
(c) Counting (d) None of these.

22. A computor is called digital on the basis of :
(a) Size and capacity (b) Operating principle
(c) Application (d) All of these.

23. The external data storage device includes :
(a) Floppy disk (b) Magnetic drum
(c) Magnetic tape (d) All of these.

24. The most widely used external storage device is :
(a) Magnetic tape (b) Magnetic drum
(c) Floppy disk (d) Punch cards.

25. The floppy diskettes are available in the size of :
(a) 8 Inch (b) 5.25 Inch
(c) 3.5 Inch (d) All of these.

26. The internal storage device refers to :
(a) Hard disk (b) Winchester disk
(c) Floppy disk (d) (a) and (b).

27. Hard disks are available in the size of :
(a) 14 Inch (b) 10.5 Inch
(c) 8 Inch (d) All of these.

28. Hardware refers to :
(a) Central Processing Unit (b) Monitor
(c) Printer (d) All of these.

29. A binary digit, 0 and 1 refers to :
(a) Byte (b) Bit
(c) Nibble (d) None of these.

30. Byte refers to a group of :
(a) Four bits (b) 8 bits
(c) Ten bits (d) 12 bits.

31. Nibble refers to a group of :
(a) Four bits (b) Eight bits
(c) Ten bits (d) 12 bits.

32. A group of program refers to :
(a) Software (b) Hardware
(c) Nibble (d) None of these.

33. Read/write memory is also called :
(a) RAM (b) User memory
(c) ROM (d) (a) and (b).

34. The Microprocessor includes :
(a) Arithmetic logic unit (b) Register unit
(c) Control unit (d) All of these.

35. The peripherals refer to :
(a) Input devices (b) Output devices
(c) (a) and (b) (d) None of these.

36. Input devices refers to :
(a) Keyboard (b) Monitor
(c) Printer (d) All of these.

37. Output devices include :
(a) Monitor (b) Printer
(c) (a) and (b) (d) Keyboard.

38. A group of four bits is called :
(a) Bytes (b) Nibbles
(c) Program (d) None of these.

39. A group of eight bits is known as :
(a) Program (b) Nibble
(c) Bytes (d) Software.

40. The portable computer refers to :
(a) Laptop (b) Palmtop
(c) (a) and (b) (d) Mini computer.

D. FILL IN THE BLANKS

1. Computers are .... devices of data processing.
2. Digital computers operate by ....
3. Analog computers operate by ....
4. Hybrid computers operate by ....
5. Microcomputers are built with ....
6. Microcomputers are designed for use by ....

7. Microcomputers are also called ....
8. Mini computers can serve ....
9. Storage capacity of mainframes is ....
10. Storage capacity of super computers is ....
11. Vacuum tube is used in .... computers.
12. Transisters are used in .... computers.
13. Integrated circuits are used in .... computers.
14. Large scale integrated circuits are used in .... computers.
15. Airconditioning is not required for .... computers.
16. First generation computers were developed during ....
17. During 1956-1966 ....computers were developed.
18. Third generation computers were developed during ....
19. A microprocessor is a .... device
20. The physical components of computer refer to ....
21. A group of programs refer to ....
22. A group of 8 bits is called ....
23. A group of 4 bits is known as ....
24. Input device includes ....
25. Output devices include ....
26. Input and output devices are called ....
27. The smallest size computer is called ....
28. Floppy disks are used as .... storage devices.
29. Winchester disk refers to ....
30. Peripherals refers to .... devices.

E. MARK TRUE OR FALSE

1. Computers are electronic devices of data processing.
2. Micro computers are designed for multiplo users
3. Micro computers are also called personal computer.
4. Digital computers operate by measuring.
5. Analog computers operate by counting.
6. Mini computers are designed for use by one person at a time.
7. Vacuum tube is used in first generation computers.
8. Transistor is used in second generation computers.
9. Third generation computers have LIC chips.
10. Fourth generation computers have IC chips.
11. For second generation computers airconditioning is not required.
12. First generation computers were developed in 1956-1965.

13. A microprocessor is a semiconductor device.
14. Random access memory is also called users memory.
15. The information stored in RAM can not be altered.
16. The information stored in ROM can be altered.
17. Monitor and printer are output devices.
18. Keyboard is input device.
19. Floppy disk is used as internal storage device.
20. Hard disk is also called Winchester disk.
21. Software refers to a group of programs.
22. Byte refers to a group of 4 bits.
23. Nibble refers to a group of 8 bits.
24. Peripherals refer to input and output devices.
25. Palmtop is the smallest computer.
26. The speed of main frame computers is lower than that of super computer.
27. The storage capacity of super computers is higher than main frames.
28. Hybrid computers operate by counting and measuring.
29. Viruses do not pose problems in computers.
30. Computers have automation capacity.

F. USE APPROPRIATE TERM

1. An electronic device used for data processing.
2. Computers meant for use by single user at a time.
3. A group of 8 bits.
4. A binary digit 0 and 1.
5. A group of 4 bits.
6. A semi conductor device manufactured using LIC chips.
7. A disk which is permanently fixed in the computer.
8. A disk used for external storage of data.
9. A set of instructions which a computer can follow to accomplish a given task.
10. A group of programs.
11. The physical components of computer.
12. A medium which can store binary information.
13. A memory that stores binary information permanently.
14. A group of bits the computer can recognise and process at a time.

ANSWERS

MULTIPLE CHOICE

1. (b) Palmtop
2. (a) One
3. (b) Medium
4. (c) Large
5. (d) Extremely high

6. (d) LIC chips
7. (a) Electrostatic tubes
8. (c) Main frames
9. (b) Micro computer
10. (b) 1940s
11. (a) First generation
12. (b) 1956-1965
13. (d) Fourth generation
14. (d) Fourth generation
15. (c) Fourth generation
16. (d) All of these
17. (c) 10 Times
18. (d) All of these
19. (a) Counting
20. (a) Measuring
21. (a) Counting and measuring
22. (b) Operating principle
23. (d) All of these
24. (c) Floppy disk
25. (d) All of these
26. (d) (a) and (b)
27. (d) All of these
28. (d) All of these
29. (b) Bit
30. (b) 8 bits
31. (a) Four bits
32. (a) Software
33. (d) (a) and (b)
34. (d) All of these
35. (c) (a) and (b)
36. (a) Keyboard
37. (c) (a) and (b)
38. (b) Nibble
39. (c) Bytes
40. (c) (a) and (b)

FILL IN THE BLANKS

1. Electronic
2. Counting
3. Measuring
4. Counting and measuring
5. Micro processor
6. One person
7. Personal computers
8. Users
9. Large
10. Extremely large
11. First generation
12. Second generation
13. Third generation
14. Fourth generation
15. Fourth generation
16. 1946-1955
17. Second generation
18. 1966-1975
19. Semi conductor
20. Hardware
21. Software
22. Byte
23. Nibble
24. Keyboard
25. Monitor and Printer
26. Peripherals
27. Palmtop
28. External
29. Hard disk
30. Input and output derives

TRUE OR FALSE

1. True	2. False	3. True
4. False	5. False	6. False
7. True	8. True	9. False
10. False	11. False	12. False
13. True	14. True	15. False
16. False	17. True	18. True
19. False	20. True	21. True
22. False	23. False	24. True
25. True	26. False	27. True
28. True	29. False	30. True

APPROPRIATE TERM

1. Computer
2. Micro computer or Personal computer
3. Byte
4. Bit
5. Nibble
6. Micro processor
7. Hard disk
8. Floppy disk
9. Program
10. Software
11. Hardware
12. Memory
13. ROM
14. Word

●●●

Appendices

1. CONTRIBUTION OF SOME BIOMETRICIANS

Name of Scientist and year	*Concept developed*	*Book(s) Authored*
Sir Galton	Used regression coefficient to find out relationship between heights of fathers and sons	—
R.A. Fisher	Analysis of variance Experimental designs Test of significance for small samples Provided initial frame of biometrics	1. Statistical methods for research workers 2. Statistical methods and scientific inference. 3. Statistical Tables for Biological, Agricultural and Medical Research. 4. Designs of Experiments
Frank Yates	Orthogonality Confounding Lattice designs	1. The design and analysis of factorical experiments. 2. Statistical Tables....... 3. Experimental Designs.
Karl Pearson	Chi-square test Co-efficient of variation	1. Tables for statisticians and biometricians. 2. Tables of incomplete gamma function. 3. Tables of incomplete Beta function.
Sewall Wright	Genetic Drift Mating systems Path analysis	—
Johanson H.W.	Genotypic and Phenotypic Correlations in Soybean	—
Deway and Lu	First used Path analysis in crested wheat grass	—

Federer	Augmented Design	Experimental Designs-Theory and Applications.
Finlay and Wilkinson	Model for stability Analysis (1963)	—
Eberhart and Russell	Model for stability analysis (1966)	—
Perkins and Jinks	Stability analysis model (1968)	—
Freeman and Perkins	Stability analysis model (1971)	—
Anderson	Metroglyph analysis (1957)	—
Comstock and Robinson	North Caralina designs (1948, 1952)	—
Rawlings and Cokerham	Triallel and Quadriallel analysis (1962)	—
Kempthorne	Partial diallel cross, Line × tester cross, Restricted selection index	1. Designs and Analysis of experiments. 2. An introduction of genetic statistics.
Kearsey	Triple Test cross analysis	—
Jinks	Generation mean Analysis, Graphical Method of diallel analysis, stability model	Biometrical genetics—as coauthor with Mather.
Hayman	Graphical approach of diallel cross analysis, Generation mean analysis	—
Griffing	Numerical approach of diallel analysis	—
Smith, H.F.	Classical selection index	—
Falconer	—	Introduction of Quantitative Genetics.
Mather, K.	Generation mean analysis Scaling Test	Biometrical Genetics.
Mahalanobis P.C.	D^2 statistics	—
C.R. Rao	Suggested use of D^2 statistics for assessment of genetic diversity in plant breeding populations	Advanced statistical methods in Biometrical Research.
Singh R.K.	—	Biometrical methods in Quantitative Genetic Analysis.
Singh P. and Narayanan S.S.	—	Biometrical Techniques in Plant Breeding.

2. LIST OF SOME IMPORTANT BOOKS OF STATISTICS AND BIOMETRICS.

A. STATISTICS

1. Chandel S.R.S. 1993. A Hand Book of Agricultural Statistics. 3rd ed. Achal Prakashan Mandir, Kanpur, (India).
2. Das, M.N. and Giri, N.C. 1986. Designs and Analysis of Experiments. 2nd ed, Willy Eastern Limited, New Delhi.
3. Elhance, D.N. and Elhance, V. 1990. Fundamentals of Statistics Kitab Mahal, New Delhi.
4. Gupta, S.K. and Kapoor, V.K. 1993. Fundamentals of Mathematical Statistics. S. Chand and Sons, New Delhi.
5. Rao, C.R. 1952. Advanced Statistical Methods in Biometrical Research. Willey and Sons, New Delhi.
6. Singh, S., Singh, T.P., Bansal, M.L. and Kumar, R. 1991. Statistical Methods for Research Workers. Kalyani Publishers, New Delhi.
7. Panse, V.G., Sukhatme, P.V. 1985. Statistical Methods for Agricultural Workers. ICAR Publication, New Delhi.
8. Fisher, R.A. 1970. Statistical Methods for Research Workers 14th edn. Obver and Boyd, London.

B. BIOMETRICS

9. Falconer, D.S. 1989. Introduction to Quantitative Genetics 3rd ed. Longman, New York.
10. Hallauer, A.R. and Miranda, J.B. 1981. Quantitative Genetics in Maize Breeding. Iowa State Uni. Press Ames. USA.
11. Kempthorne, O. 1957. An Introduction to Genetic Statistics. John Wiley and Sons Inc, New York.
12. Mather, K. 1949. Biometrical Genetics, Methuen and Co. Ltd. London.
13. Mather, K. and Jinks, J.L. 1971. Biometrical Genetics Chapman and Hall, London.
14. Singh, P. and Narayanan, S.S 2000. Biometrical Techniques in Plant Breeding 2nd ed. Kalyani Publishers, New Delhi.
15. Singh, R.K. and Choudhary, B.D. 1985. Biometrical Methods in Quantitative Genetic Analysis 2nd ed. Kalyani Publishers, New Delhi.

3. LIST OF SOME TECHNICAL TERMS COMMONLY USED IN QUANTITATIVE GENETICS.

Technical Term	*First used/coined by*	*Year*
A. Adaptability	Dobzhansky	1968
Analysis of Variance	Fisher	—
Augmented Design	Federer	1956
B. Biparental Cross	Comstock and Robinson	1948
Biometrics	Fisher	1918

C. Coadaptation Coefficient of Variation Classical Selection Index Correlation	Dobzhansky Karl Pearson Smith Karl Pearson	1956 — 1936 —
D. Diallel D^2 Statistics Disruptive Selection Dominant	Yates Mahalonobis Mather Mendel	1947 1928 1948 1865
E. Epistasis Environmental Variance	Beteson Burton	1907 1952
F. Five Parameter Model Flexibility Free Variability	Hyman Thoday Mather	1958 1953 1943
G. Gene Gene Pool General Selection Index Generation Mean Genotype Genotypic Variation Genetic Homeostasis Genetic Polymorphism Graphical Approach	Johannsen Dobzhansky Hanson and Johanson Hayman, Jinks and Jones Johannsen Burton Lerner Ford Hayman	1909 1951 1957 1958 1909 1952 1954 1974 1954
H. Hertability	Lush	1941
I. Inbreeding Coefficient	Wright	1922
J. Joint Scaling Test	Cavalli	1952
K. Kinetochore	Schrader	1936
L. Linex Tester Cross	Kempthorne	1957
M. Macro-environment Mendelian Population Metroglyph Analysis Micro-environment	Comstock and Moll Dobzhansky Anderson Comstock and Moll	1963 1935 1957 1963
N. Null Hypothesis Numerical Approach-diallel	Fisher Griffing	— 1956
O. Oligogenic Overdominance	Mather Hull	1941 1945
P. Partial Diallel Path Analysis Phenotype	Kempthorne Wright Johannsen	1957 1921 1909

Phenotypic Variation	Burton	1952
Polygenic	Mather	1941
Population	Johannsen	1903
Potential Variability	Mather	1943
Pureline	Johannsen	1903
Q. Quadriallel	Rawlings and Cokerham	1962
R. Regression Coefficient	Galton	—
Restricted Selection Index	Kempthorne and Nordskog	1959
S. Scaling Test	Mather	1949
Selection	Darwin	1858
Selection Differential	Lush	1945
Six Parameter Model	Hayman	1958
T. Test Cross	Bridges	1934
Three Parameter	Jinks and Jones	1958
Model		1962
Triallel Cross	Rawlings and Cokerham	1968
Triple Test Cross	Kearsey and Jinks	1981
Trans Genic	Gordon and Ruddle	
V. Variance, Additive	Fisher	1918
Variance, Dominance	Fisher	1918
Variance, Epistatic	Fisher	1918
X. Xenia	Focke	1881
X^2 Test	Pearson	—
Y. Y-Chromosome	Wilson	1909
Z. Zygote	Bateson	1902

●●●